WARRIOR

Arise!

LIVE BRAVELY, FREELY, AND AUTHENTICALLY **YOU**

CONNIE JONES

Warrior Arise!: Live Bravely, Freely, and Authentically YOU
Published by Lionheart House
Peachtree City, GA

ISBN: 978-0-578-86199-9
SELF-HELP / Personal Growth / Success

Cover and Interior Design by Victoria Wolf, wolfdesignandmarketing.com

QUANTITY PURCHASES: Bible study groups, churches, book clubs, and other organizations may qualify for special terms when ordering quantities of this title. For information, email: conniej@arisecounselingandcoaching.com.

This book is dedicated to the brave Warriors
who dare to battle for their heart
so they can live free and fully alive!

CONTENTS

PART THREE: WARRIOR ARISE!

PREFACE

"I have come to give you everything in abundance, more than you expect—life in its fullness until you overflow."

—John 10:10b *(TPT)*

THIS IS MY STORY–the journey of my heart.

I share the story of my heart to offer you wisdom and hope. It is my prayer that with God's help and your courage, you will conquer the fears and lies that hold you in bondage. I pray you will break free from your emotional prisons and ineffective patterns of thinking and behavior, and thrive in the life God designed for you.

It's ironic that I'm sharing my story with you because I'm the girl who never wanted my story. I wanted other people's stories—the happy, successful, famous ones who looked like they had done it all right. I wanted their lives, comparing myself and my small story to their glamorous fame and success. I idealized their perfection while considering myself a failure. The constant comparisons tormented me.

From as early as I can remember, I thought there was something wrong with me. Who I was had no value. Things I loved didn't matter. What other people expected was the priority. On this treacherous road of people-pleasing, I smothered my heart. I abandoned my dreams to do what was expected, following all the strategic formulas for success. I thought if I did everything right, people would choose and cherish me. God would bless me.

Growing up, I thought if I made all A's, was skinny and fit, had pretty clothes, was a good athlete, and the boys liked me, then I would feel valuable and be happy. If I was a "good Christian," a "good girl" who "did everything right," then people would approve of me. If I was nice to everybody, did what they wanted me to do, and became who they needed me to be, then they would love me.

My dreams included the whole myth: marrying the right person, having the right house, raising the picture-perfect family. It was about achievement, money, and success.

I reached for recognition in any way I could, but nothing I did to prove my worth was ever enough. There was always more to achieve, more to get, and more to improve. It was endless. The cycle kept me on a hamster wheel. I beat myself up for "not getting it right," struggling in misery, internal conflict, and defeat every day.

In this constant striving, I developed severe anxiety and became clinically depressed. I lost and gained an enormous amount of weight, earning me a stay in an eating disorder treatment center. I bounced between addictions, trading food and exercise for workaholism. Along this rocky road, I lost my identity and my dreams for my future. Instead of having the perfect life I imagined, I struggled to make ends meet on my own as a single woman. The result was a life wrought with pain, disappointment, loss, deep sadness, bitterness, and despair.

I wrestled with God… where was He? I knew He loved me but I didn't feel like He did. I felt like God had forgotten about me. He was absent. I couldn't feel Him, I didn't think that He was for me. I really thought that He had made me flawed, that He loved everybody else except me.

After more than twenty-five years of intensive personal counseling, coaching, and spiritual mentoring, I finally understand that life isn't about performance, achievement, people-pleasing, or people-serving, and that hating myself isn't the answer. Nothing is wrong with me. I am perfectly and wonderfully made by the Creator Himself. I am not the problem, nor am I "too much." I am "enough."

I realize now that God was loving me the entire time, in every situation, through all the events and experiences I will share with you. He sees me as His beloved daughter, powerful beyond measure, and He loves me.

I have learned how to heal and recover my heart, silence the voices of fear and self-doubt, and live powerfully in my purpose. I have eliminated limiting mindsets and ineffective patterns of behavior that were keeping me stuck in survival mode. Now, I understand how to live in His truth, freedom, and abundant love.

Today, God uses me as a vessel to heal and restore other people's hearts so they, too, can live in wholeness enjoying the beautiful life that He offers them. I fully embrace my purpose as a beloved daughter of the King, a Warrior, and I share my experiences so you, too, can conquer the evil and darkness that battles for your heart. My mission is to inspire, empower, and equip you to step into your true identity and live out your destiny.

The truth is that the life of freedom and fullness that God promises you is available to you. Discovering this promised land requires that you know your true identity as a son or daughter of the King and that you heal and redeem your heart from the emotional wounds and lies of the enemy who opposes you.

I will show you how to silence the voices of fear, shame, and self-doubt that keep you playing small so you can be fully, powerfully alive in your truth and unique purpose. Then you will be unleashed to live bravely, freely, and authentically in the beautiful life God offers!

Will you dare to take this journey with me?

PROLOGUE

ONE DAY, IT ALL CHANGED.

On a spring morning no different from all the others before it, I woke up to the sun shining through my windows and the sound of birds chirping outside. My dogs and cats cuddled on the bed with me, and my house was quiet and cozy. The alarm, already snoozed repeatedly, fired off again. I quickly silenced it.

Half-awake, I thought about the day ahead with overwhelming dread. Back-to-back clients with few breaks packed my schedule. A long list of emails and phone calls demanded a response, as did all the other responsibilities that accompanied running the business.

I continued to lay curled up in a ball of misery under the covers. Literally exhausted, I ached all over. The pressure to be upbeat and alert, to listen and offer wisdom and insight was daunting. Every day felt like groundhog day. If I lifted my head, I was sure I'd see weeks and years more of emotional winter.

Desperate for relief, I pondered my life. I was thirty-nine years old, still single, with no children and no family close by for help or support. I lived alone, worked alone, ate alone, came home alone, slept alone, and woke up alone. Every. Day. Success paraded its results before me all day, every day, in every way. Yet no matter how hard I worked, how well I performed, or how perfect I tried to be, it never worked out for me. I had a few good friends, but my responsibilities left little time for me to enjoy them. There wasn't much time for anything else in my life. Too exhausted for my regular practice of workouts and quiet time, those habits had succumbed to my weariness lately, too. Overwhelmed with everything I had to do to make ends meet, I didn't like my life, and I wasn't happy.

Pulling the covers over my head, I lay there hoping and praying for a miracle, something that would change my life dramatically. How did I get here? How did I get it so wrong? I was hopeless, desperate, stuck. My dream of starting my counseling business now felt like my worst nightmare. Despite my exhaustion, I had to keep going at the same pace. I was the only one who could see my clients, and my livelihood depended on me showing up every day. I was living paycheck to paycheck with no savings, no security, and no life.

Sadness and despair morphed into anger as I asked God, "How could you have called me into this work and it turn out like this? Why is it so hard? Where is the abundant, prosperous, joyful life you say you have for me, God? Because this is definitely not it."

Exasperated, I said to myself, "I can't do it today. I just can't keep going like this."

The life I planned, the one I dreamed of, seemed so far away. But what was I going to do? If I didn't keep working, I wouldn't be able to pay my bills. I didn't have another way to make a living. I had no idea what I would do, but I knew something had to shift.

In despair, I continued to cry out to God. "Why does everybody else get to have a life, be married, have children, have a nice house, travel, do fun things, have friends and enjoy their life, and I can't? Why don't you love and bless me like you do them? Why am I being punished?"

I had felt that way for as long as I could remember. I always had to work harder than everybody else and be more disciplined and productive. I watched other people hang out with friends and enjoy their life, but I didn't allow myself that pleasure. I was afraid that if I let myself relax and enjoy life, something bad would happen, or I would disappoint someone else. This way of living began as programming from my mom, but now it was hard-wired into the fibers of my being.

Maybe I would miss an opportunity or lose my edge. What if I got lazy and couldn't get everything done that I needed to? What if I couldn't pay my bills? I might be left out, or I might not have what I needed. I might be just a nobody because I was just average. So, I forced myself to keep going, striving for more, working harder. I believed there was no other choice. It was my lot in life.

That way of living served me for a while. I earned accolades, admiration, and attention, but it wasn't working anymore. Exhausted, burned out, and frustrated, I had nothing to show for all my hard work. My health and quality of life were suffering. Seeing a full load of clients for years, I had built a successful private counseling practice. Unfortunately, though, the intensity exacted a toll on my mental and physical health. My doctor had diagnosed me with adrenal fatigue, hypothyroidism, and early perimenopause.

Convinced that I had been left out of God's blessing, I saw myself standing on the outside of His inner circle. Everybody else was on the inside. How had they done it right while I had gotten it so wrong? It seemed they were all living the life I wanted. They were happy. Even the external circumstances of many of my clients' lives seemed better than mine. Some days, I felt like a fraud.

In my office with clients, though, regardless of my personal circumstances or emotional state, an x-ray machine comes on in my mind. I see and know things that help other people. This insight is supernatural–it comes from God. Yet why didn't He speak that kind of wisdom and offer that guidance for me in my life? Why didn't He transform my circumstances like I saw Him do for countless numbers of my clients? Why was my life so hard? Why did my gift and my livelihood exhaust me to the point of creating health problems? It made no sense to me. Why was I uncovered and unprotected in life as a single woman struggling to make it on my own? Why did I have to struggle so much and do everything alone? Why? Why? Why?

Ugh. I just wanted a reprieve from my punishment. I wanted things to change so badly, but I didn't know what to do or how to make it happen. I didn't believe God would help me. I thought that He had left me on my own to battle for what I could get for myself while He blessed everybody else. Was that all God had for me, to use me and my gift to help others live while I suffered inside and had no life for myself?

My exhaustion and despair were so intense that morning, I did something I had never done. I canceled my appointments. I was in no shape to see anyone. For the rest of the day, I barely got out of bed. I was angry at God, but I knew that seeking His wisdom and guidance for my situation was my only hope. No matter how hard I tried, I couldn't fix my life on my own.

At the end of my rope, I furiously wrote a letter to God that said something like:

"I don't want You to be my God. I don't trust You, and I don't believe You will help me. I don't even like You. You're cruel and mean. I don't want the life You have for me. I am afraid to trust You because I don't believe that You will give me what I want and need. I don't want You to have control, and I sure don't want You to have my money."

"I'm angry at You because of all the hurt, disappointment, and loss I have experienced. You let me wander down the wrong path in every way. You made me flawed. Is this some kind of sick joke? You stay hidden from me. You leave me out of Your favor. This whole life thing is way too hard."

Three pages of itemized frustrations continued before I finally came to a place of surrender.

"But You are God, and I am not. If You love me like You say You do, if You have a purpose for my life, then You have to show me. You have to help me because I can't help myself anymore. I am done. There's got to be another way. I am desperate. Change me and change my life, God. Show me who You really are, who You created me to be, and the life that you have for me."

I poured out my pain and anger to Him. It was blunt, real, and a relief to get all of that out.

Now, it was up to God to help me.

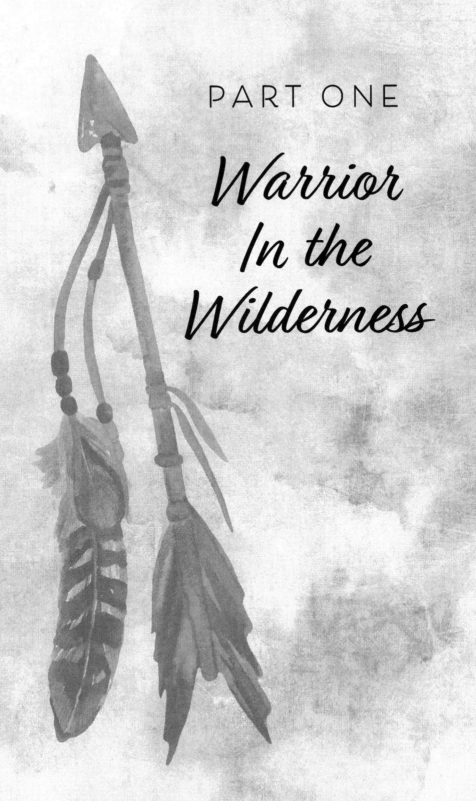

PART ONE

Warrior In the Wilderness

CHAPTER ONE

Robbed

"The thief comes only to steal, kill, and destroy."

—John 10:10a *(NIV)*

I WAS BORN THE YOUNGEST CHILD of two children to the most wonderful, loving parents ever. My brother, Philly (short for Phil Jr.), is just two days shy of a year older than me. My dad was a high school football coach and an athletic director in Georgia. He's a wise leader, a gifted visionary, a man of dignity and integrity with a heart for people and for God.

Our lives revolved around football. We lived in a picket-fenced house two blocks from the stadium. After school each day, Philly and I went to practice until my mom picked us up. The tackling dummies were our daycare. That is, until Philly was old enough to be with my dad and stand in the huddle. But I couldn't. I had to stay on the dummies.

Life as the only daughter of a football coach was tough, especially when you're a daddy's girl and your daddy's never home. I loved my daddy. I wanted to play football, to be with him, and to please him, but I couldn't.

Philly got to be with him and even played for him. Philly was a boy. He belonged. He could go in the fieldhouse after practice.

Not me. I was a girl. I had to go home early. When he joined my dad riding the football bus to games, I was devastated.

"I want my daddy," I would cry to my mom. "Why can't I go with my daddy?"

"I know, honey, I'm sorry," she would hug me and say. "He'll be home soon."

I told myself it was okay because football was more important, and I believed it. Football was always more important. It was the most important thing in life. Football was life, and football was family.

You see, football coaches in Georgia at the high school and college level, where my dad later coached, are revered. They are like gods. As the youngest child, and a girl no less, my only identity was as Coach Jones' daughter and Philly's little sister, so I had to step up to the plate and live up to what was expected of me. I assumed my place in the background, and I followed the rules.

My dad was like Moses. He redeemed a football program from years of losing seasons and poor leadership and reestablished spirit and unity in the community. People came from all over the state just to hear the motivational talks he gave his players. He was so admired and respected by everyone, including me, but that came with a load of pressure on us as his family.

Adopted as a baby, Dad had suffered emotional and physical abuse from his adoptive father when he was growing up. He found his value in athletics and later in coaching and loving kids who needed someone to teach and love them the way he wished he had been loved as a child. I loved my daddy's heart for those kids.

I know he loved me dearly, mind you, but there was so much pressure on him to perform and build a program. He was also coping with his own pain, looking for his value in his success as a coach.

THE HOME TEAM

Dad was always at football meetings or practice, watching film from games, or speaking somewhere in the community, so my mom ran our household. She also taught math at the high school where my dad was the coach. An amazing teacher at home, too, Mom taught Philly and me how to do everything. She made sure that we had incredible experiences and insisted that we be well-rounded in education, travel, music, and sports. She taught us how to manage ourselves and our lives.

An incredibly intelligent, strong-minded woman, my mom had committed her life to being a wife and a mother because my dad's job was all-encompassing and demanding in every way. We all knew the sacrifice that she had made. She had such high expectations that she often felt disappointed in how her life had turned out. She never quite said it like that, but we knew.

My mom loved me fiercely, too, but her pain was that she was the oldest child of a Navy captain who was also an alcoholic and abusive, and she craved the love and security of a family of her own like she had never had as a child. Because of her own childhood pain of not having the family she wanted and needed, our family had become her world and, sadly, her god.

My brother and I became the focus of all of my mom's attention. We were her projects. She is one of the most selfless, loving, giving women on this earth, but she made it clear how she expected everything to be at home and in public and did not tolerate anything less than par. I learned quickly that accomplishing things, achieving, being productive, and performing is what earned her love and acceptance, so I became proficient at all of these.

Mom and I were very different, so it seemed to me that she didn't like me very much. I felt like she wanted a different daughter. I was afraid and anxious about disappointing or upsetting her and unknowingly assumed the burden of making life better for her. When she was upset or not happy, I felt like it was my fault, and I would adjust my attitude or my behavior accordingly until I pleased her. As a result, I learned that I was responsible for everybody's negative feelings, and whenever anyone was upset or had conflict, it was my fault, and it was mine to fix.

Philly was the hero of our family, next to my dad. He was a brilliant mathematical mind, a natural high achiever, charismatic, good looking, funny, super disciplined, and good at everything he did. Everything came easy for him, and he did it all well. He never had a desire to do anything but the right thing. He was disciplined and driven to be the best at everything. In high school, he was the star quarterback, a talented baseball player, the valedictorian, president of the Fellowship of Christian Athletes, and student council representative. I thought of him like Jesus. I guess, in a sense, to me, he was.

I felt like I was in my brother's way. I was a girl. I couldn't play football. He didn't want me in his space, and I wasn't allowed in his room. He often made fun of me, calling me a fat pig and a mess all the time. I was always the butt of his humor.

He regularly did things to criticize or antagonize me. When I was a baby, he would rock me in my cradle so hard that I fell out and hit the floor. When we were older, he drew a line in the seat of the car and dared me to come across it. When I was in high school, I would lay out in the sun on a semi-flat roof outside one of our bathroom windows. On one occasion, he came along and locked the window so I could not get back into the house.

In any contest between us, he was vicious. Whether it was board games, cards, or other competitions, he would do anything to win. He would taunt me, trying to make me mad, and then he'd giggle and laugh about it. He was ruthless.

When I was around ten or eleven years old, I had my ears pierced for the second time. The first time they became infected, I eventually had to remove the earrings and allow the holes in my lobes to close. It turns out I was so allergic to metals, I couldn't even wear fourteen karat gold. The second time, I had special starter posts and earrings. Not long after the second piercing, my brother wanted to race in the yard. I was beating him, and at the last minute, just before we went over the finish line, he pulled back my head and ripped my new earrings out of my ears.

These kinds of things often happen between siblings, but I was a sweet, sensitive kid. I loved him so much, and I didn't understand why he wanted to be so mean to me. I think my brother loved me, but it never felt like it. As his younger sister, I was a thorn in his flesh. He seemed irritated by my sheer existence. I didn't know that he had a lot of pressure on him, too, in our family. I just thought I was his problem. I thought I was everybody's problem. I felt like a disappointment to my family, so I knew I had better whip myself into shape to try to keep up with the Joneses.

I wasn't a disciplined person or naturally thin and lean like my brother and my mom. I was strong and athletic, but I didn't care about that. I loved music, dancing, being with friends, coloring, fashion, Cheetos, chocolate ice cream–but that stuff was not productive. It was not valued in my family.

My mom made it clear that I needed to be more disciplined, more productive, more like her, more like my brother. Philly's reaction to me told me that, too, and my dad wasn't there to say anything otherwise. I knew my parents loved me, but I never felt like anybody really "liked" me. My dad didn't make time for me. It seemed like my mom didn't really like "who" I was.

My truth became this: honoring my needs and feelings over someone else's was selfish. It wasn't okay for me to have what I needed or wanted. I existed to please and make other people happy—especially my mom. As a result, I learned to take on other people's disappointments, to take care of them, and to honor their needs over mine. That became my job, my burden, my whole sense of value, and I lived in fear of retribution if I didn't play that role.

Growing up in a devout Christian family, I thought my relationship with God was rock solid. I knew that I was supposed to love God, be a good girl, obey my parents and others in authority, and be nice to everybody. So that's what I did. I followed all the rules. I was too scared to mess up in any way.

We were there every time the doors were open at the First Baptist Church, where my dad was a deacon and where everybody knew our family. There were high expectations of the head football coach and his family. After all, my dad was mentoring everyone's children as a Christian coach in the high school football program.

Our family was a tight unit, and we were always together. We did devotionals with each other, said the blessing at every meal, ate dinner as a family every night. We had fun together and shared a lot with each other, but there was no room for authentic connection or sharing your heart. We had an image to uphold and that took a lot of time and energy.

BATTLE ZONE

The first casualty in this war was my heart. To meet the expectations of others, I had to reject my true self.

All of my life, my heart had overflowed with compassion for the underdog, the lost, the sad, the misunderstood, the mistreated, the left out—people and animals. They drew me to them, compelled me to help them, protect them, fight for them, and love them. I loved caring for others in any way I could.

Yet, I didn't feel loved, understood, known, or seen myself. I often wondered: "What about my pain and sadness?" "Why doesn't anyone see me?" "Why am I not lovable?"

My heart felt like an irritant, yet I knew from reading scripture that my heart is the most precious part of who I am. I knew that through my heart, I love God and others. God had created and supposedly wanted my heart, but I struggled to understand why He valued it when I didn't?

I experienced the joy of loving and protecting other people's hearts, but my heart did not feel joy. The pain of the world burdened me deeply. I knew that God loved me, but I didn't feel His love. I questioned: "Why would He let me hurt so much if He really loved me?"

My heart had caused my deepest pains, so shutting it off and closing it down made so much sense to me. I put my feelings in a closet and closed and locked the door. I knew, though, that scripture warns against hardening the heart, so it came down to this enormous lie: *there must be something wrong with me.*

ENEMY TERRITORY

A cascade of consequences and many years of therapy resulted from believing this lie. I lived in pain, darkness, and struggle until I awakened to the truth that I had been opposed, wounded, and robbed, not by God or by others, but by the evil one who attempts to steal, kill, and destroy every beautiful, loving, living thing that God creates.

Because we live on earth, where evil has dominion, we are all born into a world of pain. It starts from our very beginning. Life for each of us quickly centers on learning to cope with our pain. Not because God created it or wanted it that way, but because that choice was made for us a long time ago by Adam and Eve in the Garden. We are opposed by the evil one, who has a hatred for God and a hatred for us as His reflection.

From the moment of our birth, the battle for our heart ensues. From early in our childhood, we're wounded with lies about who we are, who we're not, and what is wrong with us. The people we are told love us most–parents, siblings, peers, teachers, coaches, close friends–give us signals, directly and indirectly, about our value and what is available to us in life. Sometimes this information is garbled. Sometimes it is false, but we accept these messages as truth and then live out of the lies we come to believe. Often, we turn on ourselves. We believe we are flawed, inadequate, that we're the problem. This emotional wounding steals our true identity, who we were created to be.

Also, because of painful experiences, we come to believe lies about who God is and who He's not. As a result, we don't know who we are in Him. We don't understand how He cares for us as His children. We don't realize our power. Thus, every day we're robbed of our inheritance, the life and love God intended for us–until our eyes are opened.

The truth is that if we ever break free to live in our fullness, we would be a threat to our enemy who opposes our very being as powerful reflections of God. If Satan can't be God, and he can't have what God has, then he's going after what God cares about. So he attacks those very things. He threatens our significance, our identity, and he tries to steal our destiny.

He also targets our provision so that we live in scarcity and lack rather than in abundance. He bombards our safety and our security. Therefore we live in fear and shame. He thwarts our connection, so we live isolated. As a result, we have broken relationships and a lack of trust with God, with ourselves, and with others.

I know because I lived it, as you will see.

REFLECTION

"For we do not wrestle against flesh and blood but against the rulers, against the authorities, against the cosmic powers over this present darkness, against the spiritual forces of evil in the heavenly places."

—Ephesians 6:12 *(ESV)*

Knowing that you are opposed because you are powerful and a threat, how does that change the way you see yourself and your life?

What painful messages have you received in your life? From whom did you receive these messages?

How have you been emotionally wounded? How has Satan used these wounds to steal your true identity and the life God has for you?

What lies are you believing about yourself and what's available to you in life based on the messages that you've received?

What have you come to believe about your own heart as a result?

How are you battling yourself?

How do you need to make peace with you so that you can live in the fullness of who God created you to be?

What lies have you come to believe about God as a result of your disappointing experiences?

How do you feel about the story that God is writing in your life? What parts of your story are you rejecting?

APPLICATION

"Then you will know the truth, and the truth will set you free."

—John 8:32 *(NIV)*

Get honest with yourself and with God, your Father.

Spend time in a quiet place connecting to your heart. Invite God's presence to join you. Ask Him to expose the lies you have believed about yourself, about Him, and about what's available to you in life. As He reveals them, write them down. Be specific.

Then, ask God to replace the lies with His truth. Allow Him to heal your heart from the piercing arrows and to clean your filter so you can see the truth about who God really is, who you are in Him, and the beautiful story He is writing just for you.

CHAPTER TWO

Keeping Up
With The Joneses

"Grace freed us, once and for all, from the lies that we
believed about ourselves under the performance-driven
system, and now defines our authentic identity."

—Ephesians 2:5b *(THE MIRROR)*

MY ALARM CLOCK WENT OFF at 5:00 a.m. every morning
during all four years of high school. Immediately, I would get up and
go for a run on the still dark streets of Winder, Georgia, before heading
to the school gym to practice basketball.

On fall afternoons, I spent at least two hours at softball practice
or games. In the winter, basketball practice replaced softball and we
played a few games every week. Tennis started as soon as basketball
ended. In addition, all year long, I fielded balls and hit the batting cages
whenever I had the chance.

I also lifted weights in class with the other female athletes at school every day and followed a strict diet. Any free time I had outside of athletics was devoted to studying or homework.

In addition to being a three-sport athlete, I was president of my class, a member of the school's student council, and president of the Fellowship of Christian Athletes. I had so many commitments to uphold and so much to achieve that there was no time for anything or anyone that wasn't productive.

FOLLOWING THE RULES

My mom ran a tight ship at home, and she let us know how things would be done. A strong woman, she controlled our household. It was her way or the highway. There was no alternative except to comply.

Mom knew exactly how to get me to do what she wanted. I always conformed because otherwise, I could not bear the disdain and disappointment in her facial expression or tone. I quickly learned the rules, and they whipped me into shape.

"Stand up straight, honey. Hold your stomach in," she would say. "It just looks awful when people walk around with their stomach hanging out!"

When shopping for clothes, she would give me a sad look.

"Honey, you just can't wear horizontal stripes. Your shoulders are too broad for that."

I was expected to dress neatly and conservatively.

"Connie, I'm just not buying you expensive brand name clothes. It's a waste of money. Material things just are not important and think about how it may make someone who can't afford it feel."

She fiercely patrolled my modesty. V-neck tops were prohibited, strapless, out of the question. Mom had rules about the length of shorts too. Shopping for a prom dress was a nightmare. "Sexy" was definitely a four-letter word in Mom's vocabulary.

She policed my eating with vigilance, too. I love bread and sweets, but we rarely had that in our house. Unhealthy foods were the gateway to fat, which in Mom's rule book was a sin as evil as laziness and mediocrity.

She watched me closely when I was eating.

"Honey, I just don't think you need any more of that," she'd say. "I think you've had enough."

We almost always ate at home. She served well-balanced meals to ensure we got our recommended daily intake of vitamins. My brother was allergic to milk, so we never had things like lasagna, pizza, or macaroni and cheese. In addition to a healthy vegetable, we had to eat a salad and a whole carrot stick with our dinner every night. My brother and I grew to hate carrots and salad so much we would try to sneak them from the table and flush them down the toilet.

Mom believed eating out was a waste of money, too, and there wasn't an array of restaurants to choose from in our small town anyway. Once a week, though, we'd eat at Burger King where Dad's status as coach earned us half-price meals. We were allowed to have a hamburger there, but we had to eat a salad, too. The highlight of spend-the-night parties at friends' houses would be the food–Little Debbies, pizza, and Mountain Dew–because I never had anything like that at home.

As soon as I could drive, I would get a biscuit from McDonald's at least once a week after my morning run.

At one point, I wanted to be a college cheerleader. Even though I had never had the opportunity to take gymnastics–it wasn't available in our community–I won a best-all-around award at a regional camp of hundreds of teens. In eighth grade, I got the highest cheerleading tryout score, which made me captain of our squad. However, going into ninth grade, my parents sat me down in their room and encouraged me to consider other options.

"Honey, we know you love cheerleading, but we want you to think and pray hard about this," Mom said. She and Dad emphasized the importance of me learning the values and lessons that result from being part of a team.

So I pushed my dreams aside to please others. Playing sports it was, and three of them to be exact because I had to overachieve. Plus, being well-rounded and productive with my time and energy was the only option.

As a family, we were very involved in our church. We all served on the Youth Council. Philly and I were involved in the church choir and handbells, too. Throughout all of my school years, I was fervently committed to God, which to me meant obeying His rules and being a "good Christian." Don't disappoint Him or make Him mad either.

The standards were clear and reiterated daily. You excel. You achieve. You lead. You be the best. You work harder than anybody else, but you stay humble. You give the credit to God, love other people, give to those less fortunate than you, and you don't take a break. You strive for perfection in spite of how tired you are, despite how you feel.

I couldn't just run around with the other kids. I couldn't go to parties and have a good time and shirk my responsibilities. I never drank alcohol, never missed school or church, never cussed, and I obediently followed all the rules, making sure to put everyone's needs ahead of mine.

I never did anything wrong and I was nice to everybody – except me.

It was clear that being me wasn't enough. Though I felt lost and afraid, I had to figure out a way to set myself apart. I had to be different, better than others. It wasn't okay to be in my family and be just an average, normal kid. The standards and expectations were much higher for me. I had to meet them or feel unloved and unaccepted–it didn't feel like there was any other option. I had to figure out how to keep up with the Joneses.

So, I did exactly what was expected. In high school, when more was at stake, I really kicked it into gear. Education was very important to my parents. Making good grades and being a leader at school and on my teams was the expectation.

A year ahead of me, my brother set a very high standard, too, so I followed in his footsteps. Before his freshman year, he declared that he wanted to be the valedictorian of his class, and he wanted a college scholarship to play football. Knowing that, I couldn't let the family down. I knew that was the standard that I had to uphold, too. The ante was even higher for me, though, because I had to prove my value and worthiness. There was no other way to live.

My mom taught me how important it is to write down your goals and your to-do-list.

"Connie, you're not going to accomplish anything if you don't have goals," my mom said.

At the beginning of high school, we sat down and wrote my goals in big markers on a poster board, then hung it on the inside of my bedroom door. One of my goals was to be valedictorian. Another was to earn a softball scholarship. Every single day, I saw these goals and I lived by them.

I wrote down everything I had to do in a day on a to-do list and then scheduled them. I noted tests on my schedule and then planned when to study for them. I planned the time I would spend writing notes from what I'd learned in classes each day. If it wasn't on my to-do list, I didn't do it. I learned to live by that schedule. I was very regimented.

It proved to be a strategy that worked. I ended my senior year as valedictorian, captain of three sports teams, Homecoming Queen, and Georgia Female Student-Athlete of the Year. I earned many awards and scholarships. At my mom's prompting, I carried my achievements around on a frequently updated index card, ready to capitalize on any opportunity for other honors that came along.

MEASURING UP

My identity was in making good grades and achieving athletic accolades, being a good Christian and a loving daughter and sister. Though my parents loved me very much, they were well-respected leaders in town. My older brother was a star student and athlete. The pressure to maintain such high standards left me feeling like I constantly had to achieve more to earn my value not only in my family but also in our community. The stakes were high if I messed up.

I quietly and obediently filled these roles but in striving to earn my identity and value, there was little room left for me to show up as my true self. Life was about performance and accomplishment, and it continued that way through school and into my career.

It didn't take me long to discern what I needed to do to cure my feelings of inadequacy. I had to shut off my heart and become a machine. What emerged from years of rules, discipline, high standards, and performance was a fierce warrior of a girl who grew into a fierce woman. I fought relentlessly against myself and my human weakness. I was my own worst enemy.

CAN YOU RELATE?

You may identify with falling into the performance and achievement trap like me, or how you sought your own identity, worth, and significance may differ from mine. We seek to find our value, our mere identity in wealth, accomplishments, success, beauty, or fame. Yet, none of those things can ultimately satisfy our ache or our brokenness.

No matter our circumstances and life conditions, we all have fallen prey to the vicious schemes of our enemy. Satan's goal is to keep us in the bondage of struggle, striving, and surviving, doing whatever we can to feel like we are somebody, that we matter, that we have an irreplaceable role in God's greater story. Until we know who we really are and whose we are, we spend most of our time, energy, and resources to get what little we can for ourselves. We live to earn our worth and value.

Keeping up with the Joneses is a lie, and trying to do so will wreck you. Trust me, I know. I lived most of my life trying to achieve enough, please enough, and perform up to society's definition of success. Regardless of the level of success I attained, it was never enough.

I chased whatever I thought would finally make me feel loved, valued, and accepted. I didn't know how to live any other way. My internal measuring stick consistently exposed my inadequacies despite my success and achievements. The inner torment was relentless.

Staying on that crazy train cost me greatly. I lost many relationships, my health, and a whole lot of joy and inner peace. Life on that hamster wheel was miserable for many years, and my bottom was very ugly. It always is in that world.

I fed my need for significance with achievements. While performing was exhausting, I much preferred the gratifying moments of accomplishment over the deep heartache of being unknown and unloved. My dreams seemed so far out of reach, so unattainable.

Was this all there was? Did God create me to make other people happy? I answered these questions with a "yes" and accepted this as truth for many years. So, I became great at performing. Until the day I failed at being perfect. Until I couldn't keep up the facade anymore.

REFLECTION

"But you are a chosen people, a royal priesthood, a holy nation,
God's special possession, that you may declare the praises of
Him who called you out of darkness into His wonderful light."

—1 Peter 2:9 *(NIV)*

What were your family's standards, and how did they shape who you are and how you live today?

Did you receive the message that you were not enough? If so, how did you compensate? How have you sought to feel loved, valued, and accepted?

What is your identity rooted in? Is it based on your role in your family? Is it attached to your work or accomplishments? Is it tied to your physical feats and appearance?

How has trying to keep up with the Joneses wrecked you?

What are you chasing now so you can have enough or do enough to be enough?

APPLICATION

"I have seen all the things that are done under the sun; all of them are meaningless, a chasing after the wind."

—Ecclesiastes 1:14 *(NIV)*

Hear the truth of my story and let it free you.

Stop your chasing. You will never catch what you're chasing after. You're not created to. If you get close, the ante always goes up, and the cost is greater.

Stop buying into the lie. You can continue to buy into the lie that performance will make you feel happy and satisfied—that you will finally feel like somebody or enough of something and find the peace and the contentment you're looking for, or you can do the work you need to do on yourself. You can discover your true essence and value outside of your performance and achievements and learn how to live by your uniquely powerful design.

Stop the madness. It's a countercultural but life-giving and fulfilling way of living—with greater success as a by-product. If trying to keep up with the Joneses is wrecking your life, step off the crazy train. It's time to take back your power and transform your life.

CHAPTER THREE

Unraveling

*"Willpower has failed me; this is how embarrassing it is,
the most diligent decision that I make to do good, disappoints;
the very evil I try to avoid, is what I do."*

—Romans 7:19 *(THE MIRROR)*

ALTHOUGH THERE WAS DYSFUNCTION in my family, we were really close. There was always that sense of security, that this was the way life was supposed to be. As I headed into adulthood, one of my main goals was to find a partner to love and build something with me. It's what I had seen my parents do. Together, in God's name, they poured themselves into a mission bigger than themselves. They invested in other people's lives and developed them. This was the picture-perfect life I wanted.

Mom's lessons in lists carried over to more areas of my life than academics. I took her advice for crafting my ideal for a husband in the same way I had for meeting my high school goals. My list of characteristics for a perfect mate was a super version of my dad and my brother. He had to be a football player, between 6'2" and 6'4", good looking in an All-American sort of way, very athletic, smart, driven, a good leader, a strong Christian, kind, charismatic–but humble and down-to-earth. I wanted him to have a vision for the future and a sense of passion and purpose. He also needed to be from a good family, to have parents who had a happy marriage, who were involved in his life and who came to his activities.

I recorded the things I asked God for in journals when I was growing up, and I held those deep desires in my heart. I was determined that I would not settle. My dreams for a husband may sound fantastical, but I was headed to Furman University, also known as the "Little Harvard of the South." The school boasted a Nobel prize winner as an alumnus and a recent national football championship title in Division IAA. I had high hopes that there were many guys there who would live up to my expectations.

THE COLLEGE SCENE

College upped the ante on my situation. I earned a softball scholarship and followed my brother to Furman, where he was the star quarterback and "Mr. Everything" on campus. My first year started out great. I focused on creating my dream for my life, which included marrying a football player so that I could recreate the only way of life I knew.

However, being Philly's little sister was frustrating. I could never seem to achieve enough to have my own identity and worth. No longer Coach Jones's daughter or one of the best athletes or students, I was a small fish in a much larger, more competitive pond. Lost and afraid, all I knew to do was to perform and achieve–to keep pushing myself to crazy limits, studying, working out, practicing, and being a good Christian. So, that's exactly what I did.

I earned all A's in my classes, made many friends, and dated a lot of guys–all football players. I enjoyed the attention, but the one guy who met all of my criteria for a husband was in love with a girl back home. Two other football players met most of my criteria, but they seemed to prefer skinnier, prettier, more sophisticated girls.

All the girls who were anybody, I thought, were in a sorority, and of all the sororities, the Alpha Delta Pi girls were the prettiest, most popular girls on campus. They were fun, athletic, and smart too. I wanted to be more like them. When I made a good friend on my softball team who was an ADPi, joining this group seemed like the next step to being a part of something important. I pledged during the winter semester of my freshman year. I thought this would make me feel more significant and happy, but the harder I tried, the worse things got.

The summer before my freshman year, I had practiced and trained hard, following a strict diet and workout regimen. My wisdom teeth were removed over the summer, too, and I had a rough recovery. I ended up losing about fourteen pounds during the process, which at my fitness level, left me looking pretty ripped. I liked that feeling so much that I actually felt a high from it. I began to obsess over buying clothes that accentuated my muscular body. So when school started, I was in the best shape of my life.

I remained disciplined with my diet and workouts for the first couple of months of my freshman year. I ate whole-grain cereal for breakfast, grilled chicken salad for lunch, and cereal for dinner. But the food in the cafeteria at Furman was hard to pass up.

Released from my mother's strict diet control, freshman freedom for me meant a whole new world of food. I began to splurge, first by having chicken pot pie, my favorite, for lunch on Tuesdays, but only on that day. Then I would run longer to make up for it after practice later in the day. When my family came up for Philly's football games on Saturdays, we'd go to a buffet steakhouse afterward. I'd indulge myself there too and work out extra hard the next day. A couple of cheat days is fine for most people, but for me, it was the beginning of something more.

I sat on the bench in softball during my freshman year and struggled with performance anxiety during practice. We traveled so much for softball that I missed many of the fun events at school, and I wasn't even playing. The game I used to love soon became a chore. By the second semester, my diet, exercise, and shopping habits were obsessive. Besides going to class and playing softball, I spent hours working out and running. Alternating between starving and binging, I exercised more and more to work off the calories I consumed. My fluctuating sizes fueled my anxiety. Buying clothes not only helped solve the changing wardrobe problem, it also alleviated some stress.

At the end of my first year of college, my confidence had taken a beating. I experienced severe anxiety about not being able to live up to the image I had created for myself. Determined to get my body under control, I spent my summer working out and starving myself. But the harder I tried, the more out of control I felt. My anxiety was overwhelming.

SPIRALING

During my sophomore year, my sorority sisters and I lived on the same hall, where there was always something going on. Sorority life included many formals, parties, and social gatherings. It was fun but stressful for me because the food was always a part of it. There were so many activities that, with classes and studying, I found it hard to follow my diet or exercise like I wanted to, making it even harder to manage my weight.

The cheat days were catching up with me. As soon as I began allowing myself to eat "regular" foods, I wanted more. I would raid the laundry room snack machine for one of those big chocolate chip cookies that I love so much–the kind that was soft and came two to a pack. Then I would have a brownie. Then I would get something else. I never kept food like this in my room, but I would steal food from my roommate or friends on the hall when I craved sweets. I would even break down and order pizza for dinner and late-night snacks. The cycle of starving myself and binging intensified. I would follow a strict diet for three or four days and then binge for two days. My body became so confused. Even when I ate moderately, my body weight went up because I was in starvation mode for so long.

I had a steady boyfriend by then. He was a football player and had a lot going for him. I poured myself into his life. After Christmas, his roommate moved home, and from then on, if I wasn't in class, at softball practice, or working out, I spent most of my time with him. I began skipping sorority functions, making excuses because I felt too fat. I felt guilty for not going, but the only place I felt comfortable and secure was with my boyfriend. Soon, I didn't have a life of my own.

My grades dropped. I saw B's and C's and even a D for the first time in my life. My life was crumbling.

I stayed in school over the summer between my sophomore and junior years and worked with many other athletes, including my boyfriend, at the cafeteria. The women who ran the kitchen were so nice to all of us. I served food and helped wash dishes. It was a lot of fun, but it was also the Disney World of food. The main entrees and vegetables were like your Southern grandma served on Sunday. But then there was the ice cream bar, desserts galore, scores of chips, grilled sandwiches, French fries, a cereal bar, and more. We'd eat before we served, then have dessert after closing and take whatever we wanted back to our room.

CRASHING

By the fall of my junior year, I weighed nearly sixty pounds more than at the start of my freshman year. My confidence plummeted even more.

In an attempt to counteract my continued binging and weight gain, I worked out for two to three hours before or after softball practice. The excessive exercise, along with my weight gain, created multiple health problems for me. I developed tendonitis in my knees. My hips ached. Injuries kept me from being able to play. One day my trainer and my coach pulled me aside in the gym.

"Connie, we're worried about you," my coach said. "You're over-doing it. This is not healthy."

Genuinely concerned about my well-being, they encouraged me to get professional help. Not only was my health at risk, but my softball scholarship, the foundation for my future, was in jeopardy, too.

As things became more out of control, I slipped into depression. Some days, I couldn't get out of bed. I would sleep all day. When I was awake, I consumed enormous amounts of calories. On other days, I worked out extra long and hard to exercise off the food that I had binged. This cycle of extreme intervals repeated over and over.

I barely made it through the semester to Christmas break, when I literally collapsed on my parents' couch. Exhausted from over-exercising and chemically imbalanced from my diet roller coaster, I was also anxious about being away from my boyfriend for those few weeks. Miserable and sad, I felt alone and like a big failure. I saw my dreams going down the tubes. I felt out of control, hopeless, and desperate. I was so depressed that I didn't want to live anymore. I just wanted to sleep all day and not wake up.

My parents were very concerned, but they didn't know how to help me. My mom would try to help me eat healthier, but then she was the food police when I wanted to splurge. So I hid food and continued to binge. She couldn't understand why I had gained so much weight. I was destroyed over it, and it bothered her too. Where did her daughter go?

We had a normal Christmas day with family visiting, but it was miserable for me. I binged all day. The day after, I tried to get up and exercise, but the physical and emotional pain left me completely exhausted. Finally, I got really honest with my parents about how much I was struggling. I told them how bad the binging had gotten, how much I was eating, and about all the laxatives I was taking. I told them how much eating and the fear of gaining weight terrified me and dominated my thoughts.

"My whole world's crashing and I don't know what to do," I cried, "but I can't keep doing this."

I had lost control of my whole life. I couldn't even imagine going back to school. My parents had no idea what to do, either, but they began researching solutions.

Two weeks after Christmas, I was in Arizona at Remuda Ranch, a Christian inpatient treatment center. I was diagnosed with depression, anxiety, and exercise bulimia, a disorder in which a person follows binging with compulsive exercising. I'd never even heard of it. None of us had.

In treatment, I learned what losing control really meant. When I walked in the door, my life was no longer my own. Initially, no phone calls or visitors were allowed. Meals were planned for me, and I was required to eat–and finish–what I was served. Attendants followed me into the bathroom to make sure I was not purging.

Because of my bulimia, the only foods I considered "safe" were very low-fat–fruits, vegetables, chicken, salad, etc. When I wasn't binging, I starved on foods from my "legal" list. One morning, a small container of peanut butter, maybe a tablespoon, was part of my breakfast. The thought of eating this sent me over the edge, so I hid the packet in my pocket. The bathroom attendant found it, though, and I was forced to eat it.

As uncomfortable as the restrictions were, I found freedom and enjoyed the daily group sessions. For the first time in my life, I could be myself. With no image to uphold, I could cry, scream, or cuss without judgment. It was messy but liberating.

My parents came to visit during family weekend. My dad actually missed a football game to make the trip. He had never missed a game for anything I was doing. Even when I was crowned homecoming queen in high school, he didn't miss the team's halftime pep talk to escort me onto the field. I didn't even ask him because I knew the football program was more important. I asked a close friend to walk with me instead. When I realized he had missed a game to be there, I hugged him and cried and cried and cried. I remember thinking, "Wow. He does love me." It meant the world to me.

During several family counseling sessions that weekend, the three of us shared openly and vulnerably with each other. Mom and Dad took ownership of the ways they had unknowingly hurt me throughout the years. We cleared up misunderstandings and got to know each other more authentically. Everything wasn't healed during that one weekend, but it was a great start to a new relationship for all of us.

CRAVINGS

I stabilized in the treatment center. I learned what was happening to me, that I had an eating disorder. This problem, an addiction, was all about trying to feel some sense of control in my life when things felt so out of control. I realized that I was trying to find my identity and significance in my appearance and achievements. The deeper issue was that I didn't know who I was outside of my family and accomplishments and felt I had no value outside of being an athlete.

When we don't know who we are, we seek our identity in whatever others value. We crave to be known, seen, and loved, to be enough. We yearn to fill the ache inside. It's wired in us. Yet we often fill it with a counterfeit for what we really want. We cope with our pain and feelings of inadequacy by anesthetizing ourselves with things that will bring any sense of temporary pleasure or relief.

We employ many vices for gratification or relief from our discomfort, pain, and stress. "Drugs" of choice may include food, alcohol, love, porn, sex, shopping, performance, caffeine, smoking, exercise, work, money, achievement, or other "substances." We give our energy, attention, and resources to our addictions while depriving ourselves of what we really are longing for.

Rather than filling the void, the remedies we use perpetuate our emptiness. So caught up in punishing or anesthetizing ourselves, we are unaware that these addictions steal life from us.

Can I be real with you? That thing you're using to take the edge off, to fill your emptiness, to give you moments of relief, validation, and value–it's a substitute for the connection, intimacy, security, and significance you crave. This deceptive trap of lies ensnares us.

What keeps us stuck in the cycle is that we believe it's all that's available to us. This lie robs us blind. Instead of living fully, we settle for the counterfeit, trapped in survival mode with brief moments of relief.

To end this vicious cycle, we have to connect with our heart, find out what it's truly craving, then spend our time, energy, and resources seeking this rather than mere relief. Sometimes, awakening to the truth of what we are doing and how it is not working for us is enough of a catalyst for change, but often we need help outside of ourselves to make the shift.

I spent sixty days in Arizona. When I returned home to Winder, I stayed out of school for a full year, continuing intensive treatment on an outpatient basis. My therapist gave me the hardest assignment of my life:

"Do nothing for a year," he said. "You need to heal and take the time to figure out who you are. Stop doing and learn to be."

REFLECTION

"Their land is filled with idols; they bow down to the work of their hands, to what their own fingers have made."

—*Isaiah 2:8 (ESV)*

What was or is your perfect picture? What does the perfect life look like for you?

How have you pursued your dream?

Is what you're pursuing a realistic dream or a fantasy? *(Did you read my criteria for a husband? Really?!!)*

What are your value and significance rooted in?

What is your go-to when life feels out of control?

What are your substitutes of choice? What takes the edge off, relieving your anxiety or other uncomfortable emotions?

What is it that you truly long for?

APPLICATION

"Jesus said to her, Everyone who drinks of this water will be thirsty again, but whoever drinks of the water I will give him will never be thirsty again."

—John 4:13-14 (ESV)

Are you settling for counterfeit? Are you stuck in the cycle of addiction?

After recognizing what you're truly longing for, get honest about what you're choosing that moves you farther away from that. What can you choose instead that will take you closer to what you want most?

At some point, we realize that to have what we really want, we must change.

Change feels hard, especially when our habits give us positive reinforcement. Decide today that you will not continue settling for counterfeit. You can have what you desire most. You are free to go after it.

Start now.

Ask for help if you need it.

CHAPTER FOUR

Searching For Significance

"I'll rescue them from all the places they've been scattered to in the storms... I'll go after the lost, I'll collect the strays, I'll doctor the injured, I'll build up the weak ones and oversee the strong ones so they're not exploited..."

—Ezekiel 34:12, 16 *(The Message)*

THE IDEA OF DOING NOTHING scared me to death. It made my mom really uncomfortable, too. After adjusting to this new way of being, my parents and I had a special year together as a family. The three of us grew closer than we have ever been.

Getting better was my full-time job. I slowly incorporated foods back into my diet and exercised regularly in healthy ways. Three nights a week, I drove to Atlanta to participate in group therapy and saw my counselor once a week for individual sessions. I also learned that I had obsessive-compulsive disorder, which had exacerbated the eating disorder. My doctor prescribed medication which helped manage this.

I was finding out so much about myself. In between sessions, I shared my discoveries with my parents. The more I shared with Dad, the more he realized he had some issues similar to mine that he had never dealt with. He began to get help, too. We saw the same therapist for a couple of years after that. On many days, we spent hours talking things over. It was a healing time for my dad and me. We became super close.

Mom had a harder time understanding. She vacillated between being supportive and defensive, policing my eating and activities as she had always done. She struggled to trust my therapist. We had some knock-down drag-outs as I discovered myself outside of who I had been programmed to be.

She didn't know how to respond to the change in me. She lived a life of discipline, productivity, and performance. She loved me fiercely and was always more supportive than anyone, pulling for me in every way. She helped me in any way she could, often sacrificing herself to do so. We were just wired differently. Our perspectives and the way we did things were not the same.

I think she worried, "What is happening to my daughter?" Maybe she was afraid of losing control or concerned she wouldn't have her own picture of the family she always wanted. As hard as it was, though, we talked and worked through every issue that came up. This was the beginning of a long-term healing process for us.

ANGELIC INTERVENTION

My boyfriend broke up with me and started seeing someone else after I left the treatment center. Furman had been such a struggle and disappointment for me. I felt it was best for me to start fresh somewhere else. The next year, I transferred to The University of Georgia to finish my bachelor's degree.

Fortunately, God sent an angel to guide me through the process. Shortly after I enrolled at UGA to finish my undergrad degree, I began working with a therapist whose name, believe it or not, was Angel. Her office was in Athens, and I worked with her the entire time I was in school there and on and off for many years afterward.

Angel lived up to her name and more. Beautiful, always tan and trim, even her appearance matched her name. A casually coordinated wardrobe complimented her short blond hair. She sparkled. Her office was equal parts tasteful and comforting, with light turquoise walls and a brown sofa. Her desk was always a mess, but everything else was tidy. Willow Tree angels were scattered around the room. Light poured in through two windows which flanked a gorgeous painting of a beach scene. Some of the most important truths of my life were revealed in this room.

Angel and I took a deep dive into my history. She helped me understand the dynamics of my family and my childhood. She probed the messages I received and life experiences that had wounded me, and the lies I had believed about myself that led to such struggle. She helped me recognize the layers of pressure I had lived under for so long and the unrealistic expectations that had been set for me.

Then, she helped me identify what I liked and didn't like, what I'm okay with and not, what I wanted and didn't. I discovered the voice that I never had growing up and began the process of healing so that I was no longer a victim or a child who felt out of control.

Angel taught me how to have fun while still being responsible and how to set healthy boundaries with my parents–including standing up to my mom when I felt judged or shamed. I uncaged from some of the bondage of having to perform and be perfect or measure up to expectations. I also learned how to reconnect with my body, to listen to my hunger and fullness levels, to exercise moderately and eat intuitively.

The eating disorder stabilized, although I was never completely free from the thoughts. My eating or exercise was out of balance from time to time, but I got much better and functioned well. I came to know myself and what my heart and my body need more than ever.

I learned how inundated with shame and unfounded guilt I was. Angel helped me recognize shame and eliminate it from my life. She would always tell me to stop "shoulding" on myself, that it was cruel and mean, and I didn't deserve to be treated like that. I learned to listen and feel and be me and know that I was okay, that I was loved and lovable.

In our sessions, I would always talk about how bad I had eaten or how bad I was because I wasn't disciplined enough that week and bash myself for my imperfections and failures. Angel would put it in perspective for me every time and help me be more accepting of me.

She shifted my perspective on life, on relationships, on how I saw myself, and about God. Angel introduced me to God as a Father instead of a judge or a punisher. My perspective about me and about life changed completely, and I began to feel human. Angel was an important part of my journey for many years.

Even though I was making tremendous progress with Angel, my old patterns of thinking were still a part of me. The year and a half that I had spent in treatment and therapy removed me from the environment and pressures that fueled my struggles. When my dad, coincidentally, was hired as a football coach at the University of Georgia shortly after I enrolled, I was thrust back into many of my previous roles and fantasies.

I was hopeful and excited. Maybe my dreams weren't lost. I was finally going to be somebody. I could finish my education in exercise and sport science, teach aerobics in Athens, and continue my fitness journey. And I could make sure that I landed a football player as a boyfriend to get back on track for the life I wanted so badly.

I met a football player in a class I was teaching for athletes. We began dating and I quickly lost myself in him. Having a boyfriend who played football and my dad as a coach made me feel significant and valuable. It was fun and exciting at times, but it was also very empty.

I wasn't an athlete anymore, so I never really felt part of things. I hated partying, but my boyfriend was into it and I felt like I had to live that life to fit into the scene. I constantly worried that my boyfriend would cheat on me with all of the girls who were interested in him and at least one time (that I know of), he did. He was my identity, so I swallowed it and moved on.

Despite what I had learned in the last year, I still felt a lot of pressure to look good. I spent money I didn't have on clothes to uphold the image I thought I should have, racking up large balances on my credit cards. It was a while before I realized this was also due in part to my obsessive-compulsive disorder.

My relationship with my boyfriend was unhealthy. Though we stayed together for three years, my clinginess and insecurity finally broke us up. Looking back, I realize just how lost and sad I was during those years. I finished my undergraduate degree, made some friends, taught aerobics, and enjoyed fun times being "an insider" in the football program, but I felt alone, fearful, and unfulfilled.

I stayed at Georgia and got my master's degree because I still didn't know what I wanted to do with my life except be the wife of a football player and eventually a mom. I desperately wanted to feel like I was special and had a life of my own. Thinking that I could work in the fitness industry or maybe even get a job in an athletic department, where I could meet my husband, I decided to work as an aerobics instructor and personal trainer and pursue my master's degree in sports management.

My brother and I were estranged during that time. I had lost contact with him after I went to treatment at Remuda. After college, he married the captain of the cheerleaders at Furman, a Miss South Carolina runner-up. He moved away, had five beautiful children, and created the picture of a dream life. He was excelling. He was well on his path to success, making great money in his own financial investment firm, and traveling a lot for work. He was doing everything right. The contrast between my failures and his successes made it painful for me to talk to him. I couldn't seem to get anything right.

ENGAGED

Several months into my master's degree, I met an amazing man who was to become my fiancé.

He wasn't a football player, but he was a baseball coach at Georgia. Close enough. I relaxed my criteria. He was incredibly good looking and a great athlete, that All-American guy who could give me the life and identity I wanted. He and my dad were colleagues and friends, even though he was my age, and fortunately, he was as into me as I was to him.

We hit it off and were together all the time. Finally, here was the guy who fit much of the image of the husband I was to marry. I was smitten with him. He was my hope.

Fresh out of grad school, he was beginning his coaching career. I was living at home with my parents, who had moved to Athens. I worked, went to class, and spent time with him. Though baseball took up most of his time, we were together in every free moment. A couple of years into the relationship, I moved back to Winder to become the YMCA fitness director. I commuted to Athens to finish my masters and see him.

We were into each other, but his work overshadowed our

relationship. Baseball was 24/7. It never ended and his obsession with it worried me. We broke up a couple of times. Truthfully, I hadn't quite given up on a football player either, or maybe even a football coach. Eventually, though, we settled into the relationship.

While he focused on his career, I worked, continued my education, and made him my life. When he accepted an offer to coach at East Carolina University in Greenville, North Carolina, the natural next step was to get engaged. I let him know if we were going to stay together when he moved, it had to be permanent.

One spring day after he played a round of golf, we were headed out to eat. When we stopped at the restaurant, he asked me to check his golf bag pocket for something. I found an engagement ring there. It wasn't romantic, but more like, "Here's your ring."

The next day, we met my parents for dinner, where we determined that there was only one weekend open for a wedding the next year. It fell right after the college baseball World Series and just before my dad began football camp. So July 12 was our day. We had a little over a year to plan.

All of a sudden, there was a lot to do. He had to sell his condo, pack, and move pretty quickly. Mom and I began wedding preparations. Her exceptional organizing skills shined during this season. We worked really well together. First, we reserved the entire Georgia Club, a brand new, up-and-coming country club in Athens. We planned to have a tent on the lawn in addition to the club. We shopped together for my dress and made plans for the wedding party, which included ten bridesmaids and ten groomsmen.

Nine hundred people were on the guest list.

After he moved to North Carolina to start his new job, I was beginning to see some things I didn't like in my future husband. His whole being shifted. He was lost in trying to prove himself. It was all about him and his career all the time. He was controlling, even buying a house without showing it to me. All of this was disturbing, but I pressed on.

Mom was concerned, too.

"Are you sure, honey?" she asked.

She loved him, but it was clear that he was obsessed with baseball. But when I said, "Yes, I'm sure," she was supportive. She wanted me to be happy.

A few months after my fiancé moved, I secured a job in Greenville, North Carolina, as a fitness director at a gym. I resigned from my position in Winder, packed up my sweet little rental house, and headed for a new life.

After I moved into his house, my future husband became more difficult. He had been recruited to work for a former assistant coach at Georgia, a guy he liked a lot. They'd had a lot of fun together. But as a head coach, his former colleague became very controlling and hard to please. My fiancé was frustrated, angry about leaving Georgia for this, and depressed.

His long work hours and focus intensified. The more miserable he was, the more controlling he became. We had many arguments during this time. As our fights increased, so did my unhappiness and insecurities.

One evening, I came home from work and let the dogs out. A few minutes later, I heard my six-year-old yellow lab, Luckie, squealing. She had escaped from the fence and been hit by a car. Still new to town, I didn't know where to find an emergency veterinarian. Also, my car had way more than two hundred thousand miles on it and wasn't dependable at a critical time like that.

I called my fiancé.

"Luckie's been hit by a car. I need to get her to a vet."

Though practice was over, he was still talking to some of the guys at the end of another bad day.

"I can't believe you let that happen," he yelled. "I'm at practice! This is ridiculous."

And he hung up.

I made it to the animal hospital that night on my own. The vet put a cast on Luckie's broken leg. She was okay, but my fiancé and I were not.

A couple of weeks later, we had the biggest fight yet. We were hanging out together before he left for a tournament the next day. He was in a foul mood. I can't even remember what we argued about. As usual, it ended up being about our relationship. If anyone understands what a coach's life was about, I do, but he was over the top.

"You're never home," I accused. "I moved my whole life here for you, left my family and friends, and I'm alone all the time! And when you are home, you're miserable to be around!"

I was losing patience. He completely focused on baseball and didn't want to talk about our future. We had argued about this for months, but this time he was so angry. Around eleven o'clock that night, he lost it and told me to get the f*** out of his house.

Devastated, I loaded up my dogs and called the only friend I really knew in Greenville. She took my dogs and me in for the next six months while I regrouped.

That same weekend, Mom and Grandma were addressing wedding invitations at my grandmother's home in Fort Lauderdale. Fortunately, they hadn't mailed them yet.

When I called to tell Mom the wedding was off, she was loving and consoling.

"We've been praying for this," she said.

QUESTIONING

When you hear someone tell their story about a particularly painful or disappointing time in their life, you can almost always count on the fact that at some point as they are telling it, they will make a statement that is similar to this one.

"I knew it wasn't right, but I didn't listen to my gut."

I call that the "voice of knowing."

Following Philly to Furman seemed natural, but did I even ask myself whether it was the right place for *me*?

I couldn't afford all of the pretty clothes I was buying, but the roar of the need to look good and fit in drowned out the sound of my internal warning system.

I knew my relationship with my fiance was toxic, but I ignored many warnings. I left my home, my family, my community, and my job to make his life the focus of mine.

I traumatized my heart and body, trying to measure up to my picture-perfect life.

Have you ever done this?

Maybe you heard your voice of knowing when you made that decision to get married.

Maybe when you made that move or took that job. Or when you turned down that opportunity because it was scary or uncomfortable.

Maybe you felt it when you started that new endeavor.

Maybe you knew when you made that financial decision.

Maybe you're moving forward with a pivotal decision right now, but the truth is gnawing at your insides.

All of us have that moment, often several of them in our lives, where we abandon our truth by choosing not to listen to our voice of knowing. Instead, we succumb to pressure from society, from our friends or loved ones, to the image of who we think we should be, or to the reality that we should create for ourselves.

We do what we "should" do or what we feel like we "have to" do.

We listen to the voice of fear, desperation, obligation, or guilt, knowing deep inside, it's not what's best for us.

I still desperately wanted to feel like I had an identity and some value – that I belonged somewhere. I wanted to be loved. My hope had been to attach myself to a guy who could provide the same life for me that I had always known – athletics, the coaching world, being part of a family, and having the image of that family admired and respected in the community. That, to me, meant that I was somebody. It's all I'd ever known. I didn't want anything else.

But, being twenty-seven years old, single, and feeling lost in life, I had no other choice but to finally figure out who I really was. I knew that I had to create an identity and make a living for myself. I had to let go of the picture I had carried of my future life and find my way home. I had no idea where that was, but by Christmas, I was living with my parents again.

REFLECTION

*"What good will it be for someone to gain the
whole world yet forfeit their soul?"*

—Matthew 16:26 *(NIV)*

We are taught through various experiences in our lives that our hearts
can't be trusted. We are encouraged to give away our power to impress
and please others. It may have become so automatic and so ingrained
in us that we don't even fully realize what we are doing.

When have you ignored your truth? When have you handed away your
power by choosing not to listen to or trust your voice of knowing?

Who were you programmed to be? Have you discovered who you are
outside of your programming, or is it time to do that now? If you did,
was someone else uncomfortable with that? How did that feel?

How have you succumbed to the pressure of others or society about
who you should be and the reality you should create? What was lost/
forfeited as a result?

In whom or what are you searching for your significance and value?
What is the result and impact of that on your heart and on your life?

APPLICATION

"I consider that our present sufferings are not worth comparing with the glory that will be revealed in us."

—Romans 8:18 *(NIV)*

The solution to this is not to beat yourself up for your past mistakes. It's time to learn and grow from them. You can't undo what has been done. Forgive yourself, and let it go.

Decide now to do something different moving forward. Commit to yourself that you will begin living congruently with what is important to you. Trust your inner voice that knows what is best for you.

Stop overriding those important messages from the heart of who you are. Today is the day to start listening to and gaining confidence in your own wise, powerful voice of truth.

It always knows the way.

CHAPTER FIVE

Strong Connie

*"For our struggle is not against flesh and blood, but
against the rulers, against the authorities, against the powers
of this dark world and against the spiritual forces of
evil in the heavenly realms."*

—Ephesians 6:12 *(NIV)*

MOVING BACK IN WITH MY PARENTS after my broken engagement meant relocating to Shelby, North Carolina. At that time, my dad was coaching at Gardner-Webb University. While I completed my last semester of grad school in sports management, I also worked as a graduate assistant in both compliance and strength and conditioning for the athletic department.

That next year at home was a time of deep soul searching, healing, and regrouping. Quickly I realized just how much of myself I had given away trying to meet the expectations and approval of others. Exhausted from the pursuit of my idealized image of a perfect life, I was at a new bottom.

Yet, as disappointing as it was to see that my life was nowhere near where I thought it should be, I was hopeful in the new beginning. Picking up the pieces, it was a pivotal time for figuring out who I really am and where I was going.

Having been in counseling on and off since I was nineteen years old, I spent the year delving back into the truths I had learned. With greater focus and resolve, I continued to see Angel in Athens. Since she was more than two hours away, I would drive down weekly for two- and three-hour-long appointments, and together, we also explored new truths.

Also, during this time, I reconnected with God and desperately sought Him for healing, wisdom, and guidance. I knew He was the answer–that in order to find myself, He had to show me who He made me to be. So I ventured into a new level of heart work with God as my guide and Angel by my side. Little did I know, I was headed into a war zone.

THE ENEMY WITHIN

I'll never forget the day I discovered my protector self, the part of me that had helped me survive since childhood. I first met her in an inner healing prayer session. Inner healing prayer was a method Angel used to help me connect intimately with God and experience His presence. She would help me relax deeply and pray to invite the presence of God into our session. We would ask God to reveal His wisdom and truth about negative memories, traumatic or painful experiences, or current struggles. He would always show up and speak truth, offering healing through His words, images, or visions.

It was invariably a powerful experience that resulted in breakthroughs for me.

On this particular day, I asked God to show me who He created me to be and to reveal His love for me. Despite all the disappointment and pain I had felt, I knew that He loved me because His word said so. But I couldn't feel His love. I couldn't believe He had a plan for me. A wall of disappointment and loss separated me from Him. I was desperate to hear His truth and feel the warmth and security of His presence.

Yet, this time, instead of hearing His voice and feeling His love, I saw a vision of a strong, haughty woman. Her hand was on her hip, and her face was angry. In a harsh and condescending voice, she said to me, "You're so stupid for thinking He wants to talk to you, much less that He loves you. Who do you think you are? He doesn't care. You're on your own."

For the next several minutes, she bombarded me with a list of things that were flawed about me. She told me what I had screwed up in my life and why I was struggling and not happy. And, of course, it was all my fault.

"What are you doing this shit for? This isn't real. This isn't going to help you," she said. "God's not going to do anything. He hasn't helped you so far. Look what your life is, look what you're doing."

"You come in here and do this therapy thing all the time and you get nowhere. You just keep going back to the same thing. You suck at relationships. You're fat. You're lazy. You can't manage your money, and you're all alone because you've made bad decisions in your life. Blah, blah blah…"

Her voice was familiar. I recognized it as my inner critic and realized that it sounded similar to my mom's voice but was harsher and meaner. This was the voice that had whipped me into shape and simultaneously shamed me for many years.

As I described what I was seeing and hearing, Angel knew right away what the voice was. She helped me understand that it was an alter ego I had partnered with many years ago and adopted as my protector self. Angel encouraged me to give her a name so that I could recognize when she was running my mind, emotions, and actions. The name "Strong Connie" immediately came to mind because she kept me disciplined and motivated to follow the rules and meet the high standards expected of me by my family. Soon, I realized that Strong Connie had been with me from my childhood. I had been hearing her voice in my head for as long as I could remember.

As I was more conscious of it, I recognized that it was Strong Connie's voice that berated me incessantly about my weaknesses and imperfections. The saddest part of the whole experience was that when Angel guided me in breaking my partnership with her, I didn't want to. I trusted her and liked her. She had become my friend. She protected and motivated me, making me more disciplined, focused, fierce. In my mind, she made me better and gave me a sense of worth and identity. She had allowed me to survive. I needed her.

To be clear, I am not schizophrenic. I do not have multiple personalities, nor was Strong Connie a manifested separate being. She was an inner voice that was second nature to me because of programming for many years. She was a force of my will that stood between me and my heart, preventing me from connecting with God, myself, and others.

Strong Connie never allowed me to enjoy myself. I couldn't enjoy other people because she convinced me that they either wanted something from me or they were competition. I couldn't trust anyone or let them get to know me – heck, I didn't even know me because of her.

As I continued getting to know and understand her in subsequent counseling sessions, I discovered that Strong Connie was also the part of me who was proud to be a strong, fierce, "superwoman." She was my armor–my hero. I realized just how much a part of me she had become. The more conscious I became of her voice in my head, the more I saw just how vicious she was. The truth was that she hated me. She wanted me dead, and in my most depressed moments, she would reinforce to me that killing myself would make things better.

RETIRING MY INNER CRITIC

As counterproductive and dangerous as she was, evicting Strong Connie wasn't part of our plan. Angel explained that our goal was to take away her power, to move her out of the driver's seat of my life. Before we could do that, we spent time getting to know her so I could understand why I had needed her.

Though Strong Connie had protected and motivated me for many years, I realized that she had stolen from me, too. Eventually, I saw how she had kept me from connecting with the little girl inside me, the heart and true essence of who I am. My creative, loving, playful self had been taking regular beatings from my protector self since I was a child. That realization broke my heart, but I hoped as I took the reins of my life from Strong Connie, the real me could stand up, be herself, and live her life.

For the next several counseling sessions, we engaged in healing prayer, asking God to reveal His truth to us about Strong Connie and about who I really am. During one session, He showed me a vision of my inner child. It was Little Girl Connie, and she was curled up in a fetal position on the floor in a dark room.

As she lay there with little hope or life left in her, God showed me that He was right there holding her all along. However, because Strong Connie was such a loud and strong force, I couldn't feel His love or His presence. It was relieving and healing to feel His love and comfort in the deepest part of my being for the first time ever. He spoke several beautiful, healing truths to me, telling the little girl inside me she no longer had to carry the burdens of life. She didn't have to worry about being beaten up anymore. She was free to go outside and play. Finally, she could be herself. In that moment, something deep in my heart came back to life.

Little Girl Connie hadn't played outside in a long time, so at first, she felt lost. Then God showed her an open field to run in, a creek to play in, and a barnyard full of animals. She felt safe, happy, and at home there. The little girl inside me began to share her heart, her desires, and her dreams with me. I spent time listening and getting to know her every day. The more freedom she felt, the more she played. The more I listened to Little Girl Connie, the less power Strong Connie had in my life.

During one powerful healing prayer session, I told Strong Connie that I appreciated all that she had done to protect me and help me survive, but it was time for her to retire. She had bullied me with fear and shame long enough. I didn't need her anymore. As I reclaimed my heart and my life from her, I saw her shrivel up into an old woman and, finally, sit down to rest. I knew life would be different without her. It was scary, but I felt the hope of freedom from her tyranny. Though she was removed from her throne that day, she wasn't completely gone. Occasionally, circumstances would trigger her return. But when she came back, I knew how to deal with her.

COUNTERFEIT WARRIOR

We all have a protector-self, an inner critic, an alter ego. We all have an inner child, whether or not we recognize it. Our personas are different based upon what lies we believe and what we are convinced is our answer to finding our worth and identity. But we all have this truth in common. We partner with our protector self, handing over control in exchange for motivation and the drive needed for whatever we're trying to achieve. In the process, we bury the childlike part of us that is joyful and pure. Ruthless and demonic, our protector is an anti-Christ spirit that wreaks havoc on our minds and our lives.

The self-protectors' voice is harsh. He or she is our all too familiar inner critic. It's a bully–loud, critical, judging, bitter, mean, and ruthless. An accusing voice, it is opposite in every way to God's voice, which is full of love and grace. Our inner critic continually feeds us lies so that we will stay stuck in our shame and paralyzed by fear. As a result, we shut off our hearts because we believe we can't trust it. The voice of our protector self is so loud, we don't hear the voice of God. Oblivious and oppressed, we isolate ourselves and disconnect in order to survive.

Our protector-self drives us to perfectionism, performance, compulsions, and addictions, which are all liars and thieves. They steal our identity, our connection with ourselves, others, and God, and our destiny. Because the lies are so strong and our shame and fear so great, we remain stuck in a vicious cycle. We are deceived, so we continue to battle to achieve our worth and our identity. What we don't understand is that this is Satan's grand scheme. He likes it that way.

Unknowingly, our protector self is our personal superhero, a tougher, stronger version of ourselves. In fact, this alter ego is a counterfeit warrior. We rely upon the counterfeit warrior as our rescuer, our hero, our god. We trust this superhero to battle for our identity and value. On some days, we depend upon him/her for our very survival. Unwittingly, in doing so, we partner with an evil scheme to rob us of our true identity and the life God intended for us.

We don't realize that in our attempt to earn our worth and value, we are actually at war with ourselves. We believe that who we really are is the problem–that we are flawed and inadequate. We also believe that God has abandoned us, left us out, or He is punishing us. We think we are on the outside of His inner circle, that life is up to us. Because we are on our own, we settle for trying to get what we can for ourselves. We seek relief from our miserable existence with anything we think will make us feel whole. But what the world offers us will never fill the ache of our hearts.

CHOOSING A BETTER LIFE

Over the past twenty years, God has revealed more wisdom and truth to me about this protector-self. Not only has this helped with my own healing, but it has also allowed me to help hundreds of clients recover, too. The more understanding I've gained about the counterfeit warrior's role, the more I see how our alter ego lies to us, steals from us, and destroys our lives. We buy the lies and settle for a life of bondage—struggling, striving, and surviving.

So many people live small, desperate existences, accepting that this is "as good as it gets." "Is this all there is to life?" they wonder in the quiet, alone moments. They wrestle with the questions, "Where did I go wrong?" "What am I missing?" "Why is it so hard?" "Where is the abundant life that God promises us in His word?"

With no hope or clarity about how to create transformation in their lives, they resign themselves to the same old, same old day after day. They sleepwalk through life, numbing themselves with instant gratifications, distractions, substances, or whatever makes them feel better.

Life goes on. Nothing changes. Repeat. Same stress. Same struggle. Another day.

It's hard for us to fathom that life can be different when we are stuck in struggling, striving, and surviving. It's hard to imagine that who we are is enough. We don't believe we can do what we love, that we can thrive in a life of inner peace and joy, living fully alive. It is counter-cultural and counterintuitive for us to trust God to provide everything we need to fulfill our unique purpose on Earth.

Instead, we live small, overwhelmed, burdened, and exhausted. We try to make things happen for ourselves, desperately seeking security, value, and significance. We are wired for peace, rest, contentment, but we settle for existing in an endless cycle of fear, stress, disconnection, and frustration. That is no life at all.

Angel was my literal angel. She helped me see how Strong Connie was the source of so many of my struggles. She taught me how to subdue and manage my inner critic. I learned how to put her in her place when she tried to move back in. It took some time to develop these skills, but fortunately, the foundation was in place by the time I was ready to figure out who I really was. Strong Connie was along for the ride, continuing to raise her voice in challenges I faced in the future, but she was not driving the bus. I had places to go and a destiny to meet.

REFLECTION

*"I am restless in my complaint and I moan, because
of the noise of the enemy because of the oppression of the
wicked. For they drop trouble upon me, and in anger
they bear a grudge against me."*

—Psalm 55:2-3 *(ESV)*

What pains or disappointments are separating you from feeling God's love?

What does the voice of your inner critic sound like? What does he/she berate you for? What does he/she blame and shame you for? Be specific. List them all.

Whose voice does your inner critic sound similar to?

Picture your inner critic. What does he/she look like? Be detailed and specific. Give him or her a name.

What do you rely upon your inner critic for? Motivation? Protection? Security? What else?

What lies does your inner critic feed you?

How has your inner critic robbed and cheated you?

Visualize your inner child. How old is he/she? Where is he/she in your mind's image? What is he/she doing? What is he/she feeling? What does your inner child want to communicate to you? What does he/she need from you?

Are you tired of the same old struggle and stress every day? Are you sleepwalking through life? What do you use for relief from your existence? In what do you seek instant gratification?

What do you ache and yearn for? What are you desperate for? How are you filling this void?

APPLICATION

"Since I am your loving servant, destroy all those who are
trying to harm me. And because you are so loving
and kind to me, silence all of my enemies!"

—Psalm 143:12 *(TPT)*

Are you tired of taking beatings from your Counterfeit Warrior? Are you willing to remove him or her from the driver's seat of your life? Have a conversation with your inner critic and let him or her know that you appreciate everything he or she has done for you up to this point, but he or she is no longer needed. He or she can be off duty. Picture yourself getting back into the driver's seat of your life.

Review the list you made in the "Reflection" section of the negative things your Counterfeit Warrior says to you. Underneath each negative statement, write a statement of truth to replace it. Decide that from today forward, when you hear your counterfeit warrior's voice, you will rebuke that voice with the truth.

VISUALIZATION EXERCISE

Be still and quiet your mind. Close your eyes. Breathe deeply. Allow your body to settle and your mind to relax.

Visualize the wall of disappointment and pain inside that is blocking you from feeling God's love. Ask God to illuminate it and to show you His truth about it. He may give you a word, a vision, or a picture. Whatever comes into your mind, trust that it is from Him.

Ask Him how He wants to tear down the wall and eliminate the block so you are free to feel His love for you.

Ask Him to show you how He loves you in a very real and personal way. Spend a few minutes listening to what He wants you to know and seeing what He wants to show you. Then, take time to journal your experience, thoughts, and feelings.

Finally, express the ache and yearning of your heart to God. Ask Him to show you how He wants to fill it. Commit to Him and yourself that you will cease trying to fill it with an imitation that leaves you wanting for more. Ask Him for the powerful breakthrough that you desperately want.

If you need support or guidance with removing blocks that hinder your connection with God, and/or help with getting the breakthrough you desire, ask for it. Contact me today at www.warriorarise.com.

CHAPTER SIX

New Directions

"For I know the plans I have for you," declares the Lord,
"plans to prosper you and not to harm you, plans to
give you a hope and a future."

—Jeremiah 29:11 *(NIV)*

OVER NEARLY TEN YEARS OF COUNSELING, I had done
a lot of inner work. Despite my inadequacies, insecurities, and failures,
I knew that I had the gifts of wisdom, insight, and discernment. As an
experienced trainer of athletes, I also knew that I was an adept teacher
and coach. After completing my master's degree, I continued to coach
athletes in the private sector, landing a job with a sports performance
company in a suburb of Atlanta.

In the summer of 2002, I moved to Peachtree City. Single with no
family nearby, I was overwhelmed, even scared. I was on my own in
a "foreign" land.

Walking my dogs the first night in my new apartment complex, a
young woman greeted me.

"Oh, I have a yellow lab too," she said.

From that moment, Abby and I were friends. She was in town on a job interview, planning to move to the same apartments in six weeks. We exchanged numbers in that initial conversation, and I helped her unload her U-Haul at ten o'clock the night she moved in. Our apartments were across the street from each other. A year later, when I bought a home, she moved in with me and was my upstairs roommate for eight years.

Abby became the little sister I never had. We both worked a lot, but when we were home together, we'd take our dogs to the lake, grab takeout, workout, and watch tv while we shopped online or worked on our computers–basically, we did life together. We had our own lives, but when we were home, we were best buddies. We helped each other every day.

SUPPORTING OTHERS

Helping comes naturally to me. I've always wanted to work with the underdog. My mom always stressed the importance of helping people. This was one thing that really worked in our family. We were all about helping people.

In high school, if one of my teammates seemed upset at practice, I'd seek them out afterward. I would go to their house if necessary to find out what was wrong. If they needed something, I'd talk to my parents, and we'd find a way to help. I'd take them to lunch, or whatever was appropriate, checking in to make sure they were okay.

Not long after moving, I transitioned from sports performance training to advertising sales. I went from helping athletes perform better to helping small businesses succeed. I excelled at this but knew there was something more for me.

Over the next couple of years, I felt called to help people the way I had been helped. I longed to see them healed from their pain and brokenness. I wasn't free myself yet by any means but knew that I could help others break free from their bondage. Having personally lived it all, I was empathic and compassionate for the pain and struggles of others. I didn't understand it then, but I was also trying to heal myself through healing other people.

Three years after moving to Peachtree City, I returned to school again to get a second master's degree in professional counseling. I continued to make a living in a full-time sales career while I was back in school. I enjoyed a good income in sales. I knew that fulfilling my calling required a large pay cut, but I had no idea how hard it would be.

Juggling a demanding full-time job while in a graduate program for a complete career change proved challenging. I struggled in overwhelm and soon began to slip into a dark time. After a couple of months of battling depression, I finally consulted my psychiatrist for help. He had told me for years that I had ADHD and low dopamine levels, but I resisted being on any more medication. Now, in this place of desperation and despair, I relented. I needed to be able to function with school and work, and I couldn't seem to pull out of the depression myself.

He added Daytrana, a milder form of the drug Ritalin, to the Prozac I had been taking since inpatient treatment. He explained that Daytrana was a new time-released drug in a patch that didn't cause the mood and energy swings that Ritalin did. I had heard of the problems that prescription stimulant drugs could cause, but having no personal experience with them previously, I didn't realize what I was getting into at the time. Assuring me that it was a very safe and non-addictive drug, my doctor prescribed me the lowest dose. He is a nationally renowned Christian psychiatrist who I had seen since residential treatment, so I trusted his judgment. At the time, it appeared to be my only option.

The first day I applied the patch to my skin, I felt better almost immediately. It gave me the boost in mood and energy that I needed to lift me out of the depression and to continue my progress with school and my job. I was so grateful that it was a positive solution. I felt no negative side effects, so I considered it to be a wonder drug. I couldn't believe I resisted trying it for so many years.

Over the next several months though, the surge in energy and mood it gave me became my solution to working harder and longer. It also enabled me to eat whatever I wanted while maintaining a low weight. I didn't realize at this point that it was an unhealthy chemical boost because I never felt high from it. I just felt normal but a little more energetic, motivated, and focused. I felt good–like I hadn't felt in years. This burst lasted for several years, allowing me to achieve new levels of success.

After three of the most demanding years of my life and a ten-month unpaid internship, I completed my master's in professional counseling and began working for the local counseling agency where I had interned.

IN THE TRENCHES

During my internship, I was fortunate enough to work hand-in-hand with professionals in our judicial circuit to create a felony drug court program. In drug courts, judges, attorneys, law enforcement and probation officers, and mental health professionals team up to support and rehabilitate rather than imprison addicted offenders. After graduating, I joined the team, quickly becoming the lead therapist and later the clinical director of our four-county circuit's drug court.

For the next ten years, I worked incessantly. My role included being responsible for a team of a half dozen mental health professionals. Together, we managed every area of the participants' lives. At any given time, we had forty or fifty people in the program who were completely rehabilitating themselves. Many were having to start over in life. During the two-year program, participants were required to get jobs and find healthy living environments. They participated in individual, family, and group counseling for ten hours each week. They were also required to undergo drug tests, comply with curfews, perform community service, and pay fines.

Our team checked curfews, worked with employers, and communicated with the drug court coordinator and drug testing vendor to ensure no one missed a drug test. I saw twelve to fifteen of these participants in individual counseling sessions weekly and ran group sessions three nights a week. Frequently, clients were texting or calling me daily about their challenges.

Wednesdays were Drug Court days for me. In the morning, our clinical team met with the judicial team for a couple of hours. I provided a spreadsheet of progress reports to the judge and the rest of the team. Then, we spent a few hours in court listening to each participant's updates and hearing the judge's feedback.

The idea was to keep participants in treatment long enough to be successful once they graduated from the program. Working with the drug court was challenging and immensely rewarding. I knew we were making a difference. I loved seeing our clients gain a deeper understanding of themselves, heal their emotional wounds, and break free from addiction. I had the privilege of helping them see their value, understand who they are, learn life skills, and take back their power.

While there's no such thing as a perfect success rate, many graduates of this program got better and never used again. To this day, I still hear from many of them.

In addition to working with the Drug Court program, I also contracted counseling services for the Department of Family and Children's Services in three counties. Simultaneously, I built my own caseload of private clients and I saw them regularly in my office at the agency. A couple of years into this journey, I worked with the owner of our agency to develop a private intensive outpatient addiction treatment program. Long thirteen- and fourteen-hour days were the norm.

Over the next three to four years, as the drug court program grew, I curtailed my DFCS work. Several years later, the program had grown enough for us to bring on more therapists to work with drug court participants. I reduced my group sessions to one night a week, and eventually, I saw fewer offenders for individual counseling. I became more of a director and less of a front-line responder but was still heavily involved in the program. Simultaneously, my private practice expanded.

My work with private clients included helping many of them break free from addictions, including drugs and alcohol, eating disorders, and sex and porn. Yet, as I saw more and more clients who were not in full-blown addiction or substance abuse, I realized that most of us are in bondage to something. Even successful, highly functioning people are held hostage by ineffective mindsets and habits that keep them stuck in struggle, striving, and surviving. Whether it was relationship counseling, anxiety or depression, trauma, or managing life stress, I saw people desperate for breakthrough. I quickly learned that we're all doing the best we can, but the mechanisms we employ to survive do not help us thrive.

THE PATH TO FREEDOM

The more clients I saw, the more assured I felt of my calling to do this powerfully transforming work. It was in session with my clients where I experienced God's presence and sensed His wisdom and direction most clearly and powerfully for each of the hearts and lives He had entrusted to me. I would sit with each person and hear their story, their pain, their struggle, and their desire. In each case, I would experience a sort of supernatural sixth sense that would light up my whole being, as God would download to me how He wanted to heal and restore their wounds and their lives. He would also reveal beautiful wisdom, truth, and direction to me for them. The Holy Spirit would enable me to see and love each one through God's eyes and with His heart, and He offered them hope and insight through me.

One of my favorite tools I used as a counselor was the unique inner healing I had experienced with my own therapist, Angel. Inner healing prayer had helped me get to the root of the things that hindered my personal connection with God, Jesus, and the Holy Spirit—including lies I believed and wounds I had experienced. I used this powerful tool for years with my clients.

In these inner healing prayer sessions, I was moved by the Holy Spirit to pray and ask Him to shine His light of truth and love on the emotional wounds, pain, lies, or confusion the person was experiencing. He would show up personally in the most incredible and beautiful ways to speak truth to and heal His son or daughter as only He could. I've seen Him pull out the lies and heal the wounds of deep trauma, sexual abuse, addiction, childhood pain, and so many different life hurts and disappointments. These experiences helped my clients see and feel His Presence, along with His peace, joy, hope, and victory in painful places that had kept them in bondage for many years previously. You talk about freedom!

I knew in those moments that there was no doubt that I was walking in my purpose, and I felt no greater joy in life than being able to shepherd the hearts of His people in that way. I was grateful and humbled that God had chosen me to lead His people to His heart, to His light, truth, and love, and to see them walk away totally transformed. There is nothing more rewarding than sharing incredible moments with my clients. I love experiencing that personal, direct connection with God, too. These times are better than any love I have ever experienced or game I have ever won, worth more than any amount of money I could ever make or any level of success I could ever attain. It's in these instances when I know at the center of my being that it is why I am here on Earth. It is the greatest honor and privilege that I can imagine.

I poured myself into my work, the people I met in the field, and the connections I made. I had finally found something of my own, something that made me feel good, needed, and special.

All I'd ever known was to throw myself into something that I loved, so that's what I did. People were counting on me. Helping them process their pain was rewarding, but I also was avoiding the fact that I didn't have much of a life.

REFLECTION

*"Let me be clear, the Anointed One has set us free–not
partially, but completely and wonderfully free!
We must always cherish this truth and stubbornly
refuse to go back into the bondage of our past."*

—Galatian 5:1(*TPT*)

What are you in bondage to? What are you held hostage by?

In what areas of your life are you desperate for breakthrough?

What mechanisms did you learn that have helped you survive in life
but are now not enabling you to thrive?

What emotional wounds do you need healing from?

What wounds, pain, or lies do you need the Holy Spirit to shine His
light of truth on?

What gifts do you have that you want to use to help others? In what
way do you dream of helping people or impacting the world? What's
keeping you from doing that?

APPLICATION

"Then you will know the truth and the truth will set you free."

John 8:32 *(NIV)*

Be still and quiet. Breathe deeply. Connect with your heart. Invite the Holy Spirit in, and ask Him to expose the heart wound and the lie you came to believe as a result of the wound that is keeping you in bondage and stuck in a smaller, harder existence.

You may even ask Him to take you to the memory where you first heard that lie and internalized it as truth. Ask Him to shine His light of truth and love on the painful memory/experience and the lie you came to believe as a result. Open to the new truth He wants to speak to your heart and how He wants to redeem the pain you experienced.

What is the breakthrough you so desperately want in your life? Invite the Holy Spirit to show you what is hindering you and how you can break free.

Darkness needs to be exposed to light. When light shines in the darkness, the darkness cannot overcome it. (John 1:5) His truth will set you free.

If you need or want more support or guidance to walk out this journey of inner healing and breakthrough with you, don't hesitate to ask for it.

CHAPTER SEVEN

A Cry for Help!

"When he calls to me, I will answer him; I will be with him in trouble; I will rescue him and honor him. With long life I will satisfy him and show him my salvation."

—Psalm 91:15-16 *(ESV)*

FOR TEN YEARS, I poured my heart into helping my clients and working hard to establish my practice as a therapist. After a decade of grinding labor, the counseling agency I worked for began to struggle financially. Cash flow became a problem.

Even though I was seeing twenty-five to thirty clients a week, and my clients were paying the agency, for about six months my paychecks were either late, a partial paycheck, or no payment at all. I had paid my dues and built a great client base, yet I wasn't getting paid. I never reached the level of pay that I made in sales, but I worked like a dog to get close to it. It was demoralizing, to say the least, and a clear signal it was time for me to make a change.

Ready or not, I knew I had to move the practice I had worked tirelessly to build. Yet, with no savings and doubt mounting, that felt like an overwhelming and impossible feat. It was one of the scariest times of my life. I had frequent crying sessions and daily panic attacks.

On a Thursday afternoon, I walked in for a regular appointment at my hair salon. Before anyone ever held a license in counseling, there were hairdressers, the unofficial secret keeper of the masses, the ones who helped people figure things out every day. She saw my stress immediately and said, "What's going on?"

"I've got to find a place to open an office," I said.

She replied, "You know what? There are two rooms right here for rent. They're next door. Why don't you call the owner? Her husband died recently, and he has owned this building for years. Call her and see what she'll do. She's been great to us."

So I called her.

My hair stylist warned me that her landlord is not the greatest about answering her phone or returning calls. Sometimes she'd have to leave messages for weeks. But when I called, she called me back that same afternoon.

"Oh, I want to help women business owners," she said. "Let's see what I can do."

So she rented me two rooms together for a price so far below market I can't even call it a steal. It was almost a gift.

I gave my two week's notice, which allowed me time to notify my clients of the move. I put thousands of dollars on my credit cards for the deposit, first month's rent, office furniture, equipment, and supplies. On a Friday, my last day at the agency, I saw clients until 6:30 pm. Over the weekend, my parents helped me move into my new office. Thank God for their help. Otherwise I don't know how I would have made it. At nine in the morning on Monday, a week packed full of clients began in a space all my own.

Suddenly, I wasn't just a booked-solid counselor, I was an entrepreneur. I had credit card debt already, but after four months with no pay and the expense of opening an office, it ballooned to $40,000. Thankfully, I did not lose a single client in the upheaval. For the next two years, I saw twenty-eight to thirty-six clients a week, taking very little time off. I had to perform to stay afloat.

SUCCESS AND BURDENS

God blessed me in what I was called to do. Clients poured into my practice. I helped people all day long. I knew I was making a real difference in their lives, but there was never enough time for relationships or a life. I was excelling at work but still fearful every day of how I was going to make it financially. I had debts to pay and could not take a break. My desire for a life seemed farther away than ever.

Abby had moved to her own home a couple of years before this. I had lots of connections but few real friends. Still single with no prospects, I longed for a husband. After long days at work, I would cry myself to sleep thinking about how much I yearned to have someone to ask me about my day. It would have been great to have someone to share responsibilities of the home and yard and to bear even a little bit of the burden of finances.

I still didn't know how to balance my life and finances. I wasn't making that much money, had student loans, and struggled to make ends meet. I continued spending money on things that made me look and feel good, rationalizing that if I was going to work so hard, then at least I wanted to have something to look forward to. I couldn't buy a new house, didn't have a husband, couldn't take time off to travel, so I bought things like clothes. At least I could enjoy wearing them while I was working.

I struggled to make ends meet. No matter how hard I worked, it never felt like enough. Every day was a scramble. It was all work, very little play, and practically no life.

I was trying so hard to make something of myself and to pay the bills at the same time. Years went by before I knew it, leaving me wondering, "Where did my life go?" I took care of my home and I worked out. Besides that, I worked all the time.

I fought to accept that I worked so hard for so little money. It was a tough reality. I ached to have a family of my own. Not only did I see beautiful families every day, but I lived in a very affluent area. Having come from a small town in rural Georgia, I couldn't wrap my mind around how these people made the kind of money it took to live the way they did. Money never motivated me, but when you are surrounded by it daily while you struggle to make ends meet, you can't help but ask yourself, "Where did I go wrong?" Twelve years later, I still lived in a tiny house, while people all around me had enormous homes. They were moving up in the world, getting married, having kids, and traveling. And I'm still right where I started.

My brother was wealthy at this point. He seemed to have done it all right. We came from the same parents. Did I miss the "how to make money" memo? I had always been able to accomplish whatever I put my mind to, but I could not figure out how to have a family, not worry about money, and live a "real" life. I just did not have a clue how to do that.

Outside of work, my fitness regimen intensified. I obsessively cleaned my home and manicured my yard. The more money I made, the more I spent. But I also paid off my credit card debt. Despite maintaining major productivity in my full schedule, I felt alone, tired, and empty inside. My workload wasn't just heavy, it was a burden. I wasn't enjoying life. I was wearing myself out but going nowhere.

By this time, I had begun to realize that the Daytrana I was prescribed wasn't good for me. Even on the low dosage I was on, what had once been an energy boost now felt more like just a surge of anxiety, which left me feeling exhausted and empty. But I was terrified of sinking back into the darkness of depression if I tried to get off of it, and I was convinced that I needed it to keep up the pace at work.

I also couldn't bear the thought of gaining the weight I knew I would gain if I stopped taking it. I believed that I had to continue the medication because I didn't have the time or margin to recover like I would need to if I stopped. I couldn't imagine not being able to function, so I kept doing what I always did–every day.

No matter how hard I worked and how many people I helped, I felt alone and unhappy. No matter how successful I was in business, I felt like a failure. I wasn't enjoying life. I was existing, striving, struggling–wearing myself out but going nowhere.

LETTING GO

For years, I was proud that I was independent, self-sufficient, and capable of achieving what I set my mind to. Early on, I believed the lie that I can't trust anyone to come through for me, so it's better that I do everything myself. So, I craved control, and I fought hard for it. That way, I could finally create the life I wanted so badly.

Though my hard work paid off in some ways, trying to do everything myself didn't work out so well. And the more I fought to be in control of my life, the less in control I felt. This crisis forced me to release my grip and to learn how to live in abiding trust in God daily with every detail of my heart and my story. I had no idea how to do that yet, but I knew I had no choice but to learn.

So, I called out to God in a more real, raw, and vulnerable way than I ever had before. I knew that was the first step. He couldn't really help me until I got gut-level honest with Him and let Him all the way into my heart, even the ugliest parts. And they were ugly. That's exactly what He wants from us though. And this is where we started this story, with the avalanche of pain and disappointments I wrote about in a letter to God.

I realized while writing that day just how much I had performed for God, too. But He doesn't want our performance. He wants our heart–all of it. And I needed some major supernatural heart surgery. I had tried everything to change myself and my life. I was desperate for His powerful transformation, and I told Him so.

FROM SURRENDER TO HOPE

We all crave control over our lives. We convince ourselves that we have it. We believe that our intelligence, hard work, good deeds, determination, resourcefulness, or even our ability to manipulate situations and people will lead to success and security. When we are at the end of ourselves, we see just how little control we have. It's also in times of hardship when we realize that control is actually bondage. Whatever we want to control is actually what controls us.

When we are open to learning and growing, we see that once we let go of the thing we are so afraid of losing, we are actually freer than we could have ever imagined. This breakdown for me was a scary but beautiful reminder of that truth.

When we relinquish the illusion of control, we create room to live surrendered to God, who is always in control because He created everything in the universe and He reigns sovereignly over every bit of it. When we surrender to Him, we can live as His children, which gives us full access to everything He has in abundance according to His unique purpose for each of us. We are no longer limited in our human ability or understanding, but are open to the more that is available to us–more than we can even begin to think, dream, or imagine.

Accessing that life is counterintuitive and countercultural. It doesn't make sense to our logical thinking. The only requirement to living that new life of freedom and fullness is surrendering our illusion of control, releasing our grasp, and spending time in His presence so we can enter into the rest, peace, and fulfillment that is awaiting us. But we must be willing to let go of the illusion of control, get to know Him and His plan, align with His heart and His Spirit, and learn to trust Him.

After spilling my heart in that letter to God, I made one more life-changing decision. I called a life coach for help. A close friend suggested the idea to me a couple of weeks prior, after I shared with him my feelings of overwhelm and frustration. He suggested that I find a coach who was doing the kind of work I wanted to do, one who was living the life I wanted to live. I considered it, but I didn't know one, and I didn't think that I could afford to hire one either, so I hadn't acted on it.

That day, I couldn't wait any longer. It was time for me to take action. My friend helped me find someone who seemed a perfect fit. I had no idea how I would afford it but sensed in my heart that it was the right move to make. I decided to trust God to honor my decision by providing the resources to cover the cost of putting it on my credit card. So, I called the coach, scheduled a consultation, and a few days later, signed up to work with her for a year.

After taking the step to call for help, I was a little relieved. I didn't hear any huge revelation from God that day, but I had laid it all out there. I turned it over to Him like I never had before. That's all I could do. Now I waited to see what happened.

Redirected from so much striving and frustration, I returned to work with renewed energy. I began to read, study, and spend time with God every day after that in desperate search of His presence and His truth because that was my greatest hope for change. Knowing that I had biweekly appointments with my new life coach for the next year gave me hope, too.

I had more healing to do and more to uncover and learn on the path to my breakthrough. The three-fold process started with leaning into God, continued with the deep inner healing heart work, and was amplified with coaching. The journey ahead of me included many surprises and "aha" moments when truth paved the road to freedom.

REFLECTION

*"Come to me, all you who are weary and
burdened, and I will give you rest."*

—Matthew 11:28 *(NIV)*

Are you weary, overwhelmed, and exhausted? Desperate for something
to change?

Are you frustrated because you feel like no matter how hard you work,
how much you achieve, and how much success you attain, it's never
enough? Does your greatest dream now feel like your worst nightmare?

In the quiet moments when you're alone, do you wonder if this is all
there really is to life? Do you question why life is so hard?

Do you wonder where is the abundant life that God promises us in the
Bible? Or how you could have gotten it all so wrong when it seems like
everyone else got it right?

What questions do you ponder in the quiet, alone moments? What
questions are you asking God?

In what areas are you desperate for change?

What do you keep telling yourself that you have to keep doing in your life for fear that if you don't, then there will be negative consequences or retribution?

What coping mechanisms did you learn early on that have helped you survive, but at this point, they are not allowing you to thrive?

How is trying to control creating bondage for you? What are you grasping so tightly? Is it time to let go of it? What do you need to surrender fully to God because at this point, you trying to control it and do it yourself isn't getting you the result you want?

What small step(s) can you take that will create a shift in your life?

APPLICATION

*"Call to me and I will answer you and tell you great
and unsearchable things you do not know."*

—Jeremiah 33:3 *(NIV)*

When you're done, when you're at the proverbial end of your rope, then what? You may ask, "Why God? Why is this happening to me? Why don't you love me?" Or maybe you question why you can't have what you want, whether God even cares, or why things always seem to be so hard.

Don't spend another moment resisting your breakdown. Stop trying to hold it all together and trying to control the uncontrollable.

Give yourself the time and space to feel the sadness, pain, and grief, then decide that you will surrender.

Decide that you're not going to continue in the same way that isn't working for you, even if you don't know what else to do. Realize that the way you learned to survive is not how you will be able to thrive.

Write out your real, vulnerable, and raw letter to God. Pour your heart out to Him. Tell Him exactly how you feel about Him, yourself, and your life circumstances. Share with Him what you want so badly in your heart. Write it down. Surrender it to Him. Leave it with Him.

Spend time every day with Him asking the questions and listening for the answers. Be still and quiet. Connect to your heart. And keep asking until He answers you. He will.

NEED HELP?

Does this place you're in feel too overwhelming for you? Do you need to reach out for help from a professional? A counselor? A life coach? A spiritual mentor? It's too hard to do it on your own, and we can't see our own blindspots.

For resources and more information, visit www.warriorarise.com.

PART TWO

Warrior Awakening

CHAPTER EIGHT

Lost and Found

"See what kind of love the Father has given to us, that we should be called children of God; and so we are."

—1 John 3:1 (*ESV*)

FINALLY, AT THE END OF MYSELF, I began to seek the Lord like never before. At the same time, an unexpected turn of events brought a breath of fresh air into my life several weeks after I decided to work with a coach. Bridgett, a friend I had lost touch with for a few years, contacted me. She, her mother, and her sixteen-year-old daughter needed a place to live for a while due to a recent financial hardship she encountered.

Bridgett and I had been in a Bible study together for a couple of years previously, and we had been good friends during that time. The distractions and busyness of life had pulled us apart, but Bridgett knew we were close enough that she could call me whenever and I would answer, and she also knew that I had two empty bedrooms and a bathroom upstairs in my home. She asked if they could stay at my house for just a few weeks until they could get back on their feet again.

Without hesitation, I said, "Yes, of course," thinking to myself that I'm gone all of the time anyway, and it might be nice to have some company in my house for a change. Plus, she said that she and her mom would help me cook and clean, so I was all for that. I liked Bridgett a lot, and I admired her as a devoted Christian woman, but I had no idea what God had in store for the next few years for our friendship and the transformation He was about to do in my life as a result.

Bridgett and her family moved in and were great company and help for me. In addition to experiencing financial struggles, she was going through a tough time in a relationship with her boyfriend. We bonded quickly over the eerily similar life challenges we faced and became very close as she and her mom and daughter lived with me over the next two years.

Clearly, God hadn't just brought Bridgett and her family to my home to provide for their needs, but He had blessed me with them as a surrogate family for that season of my life. Her mom, Carol, mothered and cared for both of us, and her daughter, Lexi, became like my own child as I shared in her life those last two years of high school. Their deep friendship and unconditional love and support helped me heal, recover, and grow in a way I never could have on my own.

I had asked God for transformation in my heart, mind, and life, and Bridgett had prayed for the same thing. God knew that the journey He was taking us on for the next few years was going to be too hard for either of us to walk out alone. Looking back, I see what a gift He gave us as He put us together during this time.

FIGHTING FOR IDENTITY

That first summer, we studied, prayed, and worshipped together every morning and many evenings, too. We were desperate for God to show up in our individual circumstances. Bridgett joined me in reading and listening to everything we could to learn who God really is and how to access the victorious life He promises us. Together, we devoured teachings on the true nature of God, our identity as His children, and how deeply He loves us.

One morning, following prayer time with Bridgett, I was taking a bath before work, and suddenly, I heard God's voice so clearly in my Spirit.

"Know who you are and whose you are, and build everything on that truth," He said.

Confident that this was God's voice, I didn't know what it meant yet, but I knew it was a foundational truth. I began to think about who I was–or who I thought I was. I had heard that I was God's child, but that didn't seem to be anything special to me. There were millions of other people in the world who were all God's children.

Furthermore, based upon my life circumstances, that wasn't getting me anywhere. For years, my life had felt like nothing but hardship, struggle, and disappointment with no reprieve. As I have said before, it seemed that God had left me out of His blessing or that I was doing something wrong to mess things up.

I thought about the only other identities I had ever known. Being Coach Jones' daughter and Philly's little sister left me feeling like I was in second place or often even in the way. I had also been the best student, the fittest, the most disciplined, the most well-rounded, and the most popular. I won those awards, but the satisfaction didn't last. There was always someone fitter, smarter, a better athlete, or more popular than me.

I had been on the arm of football players and coaches, but that ended in more emptiness and grief than most anything else in my life. I had become a counselor because I wanted to help people heal and live freely and fully, but my striving, workaholism, and scarcity mindset left me burned out, lost, and frustrated. After a few years of owning my own business, I had worked hard and was finally making a good living. But no matter how much I made, I spent all of my money trying to fill my endless ache inside. Nothing was ever enough.

As I have shared earlier in my story, I received many negative messages about my insignificance and inadequacies from my parents, my brother, and others around me. As a result, I came to believe some deep-rooted lies about myself. I got the message that just being me wasn't okay or acceptable, that I wasn't enough. Or, in some cases, I was too much. I believed that I was flawed, unwanted, not chosen or valued, that I was lazy and subpar.

My identity and value came from being who others wanted and needed me to be. What I wanted and needed wasn't important or honored. Going without was my lot in life, and I had to make the best of it.

These painful messages were arrows to my heart. They wounded my spirit, causing me to mistrust the things that were important to me. Worse, these arrows had pierced my trust in God. I had come to believe that I was insignificant, inadequate, and unacceptable. My only hope for earning God's love and blessing was in performance. So, I shut down my heart and headed down the path of performance as fast and as hard as I could.

I realized that I had been fighting to earn my identity and significance for thirty-nine years. Along the way, I had been in bondage to addictions, compulsions, obsessions, comparison, performance, and all kinds of misery. Despite my very best effort to be enough, to be somebody, and to matter, I reached the end of myself. Fear permeated my being. I was living like an orphan when I was a daughter. I was living on the outside when I was an insider. I was living like a pauper when I was a princess. I was living like a victim when I was a victor.

I pressed in to understand the truth at a deep heart level. What that meant to me was to be more disciplined, work harder, push down your heart and feelings, and be somebody else because you're not enough, or you're too much. The harder I tried to be better, the more alone and lost I felt, and the further away I was from the life I wanted to live. Frustrated, I felt utterly defeated and hopeless.

FOILED DESTINY

Satan's goal was to neutralize me. As long as I felt afraid, alone, and discouraged, my effectiveness was thwarted. This is what our enemy wants for all of us, it's why he works so hard to convince us of lies about God. He whispers to us in our painful disappointments that if God really cared, He would heal my sickness. He wouldn't have allowed me to hurt. If he really loved me, He would have given me a different story. If He was really FOR me, He would rescue me out of this torturous circumstance I'm in. We buy in every time. The lies we believe about God create even more pain, anger, resentment, hopelessness, and despair. As a result, we feel disconnected, separated from God. It feels safer that way. Who wants to love or trust a God who withholds, who doesn't come through for us, and who doesn't have our best interest at heart?

Not only was this my reality, but I have heard similar cries from the hundreds of clients that I counseled over the years. If God really loved me, He wouldn't have let my child be sick. If He really cared, He wouldn't have made me lose everything. If God was for me, I wouldn't be divorced right now. If God loved me, He would speak to me. The enemy knows exactly what he is doing using our disappointments to create mistrust between us and our Creator, who loves us and fights for our hearts more than we could ever fathom.

The lies we come to believe about ourselves and God create a filter for us. It is from that filter that we view the world and all of our experiences. It's a vicious trap. Satan uses core lies to steal life, love, happiness, and connection with ourselves, others, and God. As a result, we settle for a much smaller and harder existence–feeling left out, like an orphan living in constant lack.

I have learned that the place of our greatest struggle is fortified by our deepest lie. It is in that lie that we remain in the strongest bondage. My deepest lie was that who God created me to be, me all by myself, wasn't enough. And the story He had written for me wasn't enough either. My lifelong battle was to find a way to be enough and write a new story for myself because I couldn't trust God with me or my story. And I was willing to do whatever it took to fix it for myself and fill my ache.

At some point, no matter how hard we try, no matter what we do to get our question answered or to relieve our pain, we realize it's not working the way we had hoped. The broken things we do and substances we use to fill us up, make us feel okay, or self-redeem our story lead to a dead end. Our "drugs"–whether literal substances or endless hamster wheels of performance–deceptively lure us into their grasp, right where the devil wants us–stolen from and settling for less than God's best.

Just like the Israelites, we spend years–maybe even decades–on a journey but never arriving. The Israelites couldn't enter into the "more" God had for them because they didn't know who they were and whose they were. They didn't understand their power, authority, or inheritance as His beloved children.

But when we come to know our true identity in Christ, life begins to shift. It's the lies we believe, our skewed view, our doubt and unbelief that keep us from stepping in faith into what He is doing. When we unravel the lies that we have believed about ourselves, about God, and about the life that is available to us, we are free to build everything on that foundation and watch expectantly to see what He is doing. All we have to do is align with that and receive it.

We can begin the inner healing process, reconnect with our own heart and accept, embrace, and learn to love ourselves for who we have been all along. We can connect with God and experience His deep healing love and His transformative power in our hearts and our lives. Then, we can recognize, declare, and claim the truth of His promises for the life that is waiting for us to inhabit it. We can be completely dependent every day on what He has already done for us, establishing everything else in our lives on who He says He is and what He says He will do.

Let that ring true in your heart and mind and permeate your being. An incredible sense of freedom comes when we understand that we are made right, that we are enough, and that all we have to do is believe and receive God's truth. Understanding who we are and whose we are changes everything for us. We can latch onto the promises of God and own them.

LIBERATION

Because we are children of God, we are righteous in God through Jesus. God sent Jesus into the world to make us right, so we don't have to try to be right or enough within ourselves–in any way.

Our identity crisis is over. We are who God says we are, and we are more than enough. All we need to do is ask God to personally reveal our righteousness to us in a real and personal way so that we can stop striving to be right or enough on our own. When God sent Jesus to die for our sins, He closed the gap for us. He restored us to intimate, connected relationship with Himself, and He canceled our debt. He made us right with Him, and because we are right with Him, we no longer have to be a slave to our circumstances, to our failures, to our disappointments, to the lies we believe, to living powerlessly as a victim in our lives. We are restored to direct connection with God as His children, sons and daughters of a King.

We are enough. We have enough and there is enough. We can live in the power, authority, and confidence of who we are and who God says He is and cling to His promises of what He says He will do. We can cling to the hope and joy of all the MORE He has for us because He has done it. We just have to believe it, receive it, and step into it. Struggling, striving, and surviving are over. The pain, the loss, the disappointment–He's redeeming every bit of it as we speak. He did the thing that we could never have done for ourselves no matter how hard we tried, and because He did that, we are righteous in Him.

Now we can step into our power and live in His flow every day as the truth of what He did and is doing permeates our whole being. It is the greatest gift He could ever have given us, and it sets us free. We don't have to keep striving to create anything for ourselves. In fact, if we build a foundation on anything other than what Jesus did for us, it will crumble. It is futile.

God sent Bridgett and her family into my life at precisely the moment when we both needed liberation from years of delays and disappointments. We began a new direction together, one that powerfully transformed my thinking, feelings, and my life and, ultimately, the thoughts, feelings, and lives of hundreds of people I have counseled and coached in the years since then.

Our journey together led to momentous revelations and set us both on the right path toward an authentic life of freedom and fullness.

REFLECTION

"Because we are his offspring, we are certainly also
His heirs; God himself is our portion and we are His!
We are co-heirs in Christ!"

—Romans 8:17 *(THE MIRROR)*

What identities have you been known for throughout your life?

What false truths have you received about your value, significance, and lovability from people and experiences in your life? What messages did you learn about life from your family? How have these beliefs influenced how you've lived? What is the result?

How have you lived like an orphan instead of like a son or daughter of the King?

How have you tried to earn your identity or significance?

What substances or activities have you used to try to fill your ache or self-redeem your story?

If you receive the fact that you are an insider in the Kingdom of God, that your Creator Daddy has bestowed His favor and abundant blessings on you, how does that shift your mindset about your true identity and about the life you were meant to live?

If you believe that you have an irreplaceable seat at His feasting table, how does that change your life? How differently will you live in that place of honor and privilege?

How does this change the way you view challenges and struggles?

How does it change the way you feel about yourself?

How does it shift the way you view and communicate with God?

Try it out for a few minutes, and then receive it as truth. Because it is.

APPLICATION

"The point is this: even though they survived by supernatural means in the wilderness for 40 years, they failed to grasp what God had in mind for them. Their unbelief disqualified them. What a foolish thing it would be if we should now fail in a similar fashion to enter into his rest; where we get to celebrate the full consequences of his redemption"

—Hebrews 3:19-4:1 *(THE MIRROR)*

Just like the Israelites, we spend years–maybe even decades–on a journey but never arriving. We don't enter into the "more" that God has for us because we don't know who we are and whose we are. We don't understand our power, authority, or inheritance as His beloved children. It's the lies we believe, our skewed view, our doubt and unbelief that keep us from stepping in faith into what He is doing.

Ask God to expose the lies that you believe about you, about Him, about your story, and about what is available to you. How are these lies skewing your view of who you are and whose you are? How do they keep you stuck in struggle, striving, and surviving instead of thriving in the more that is available to you?

Spend time writing out your areas of struggle and what you believe about those areas that keep you in the battle. For each of the lies you believe, write out God's truth beside them. Ask Him who you are to Him. Who He made you. Who He is. Ask Him to share the promises He has specifically for you. Write them down. Hold them in your heart. Latch onto them and own them. Open and receive them. Thank Him for them. Trust that He is bringing them to reality.

Begin spending time in God's presence and ask Him to make His truth real in your heart and mind. Invite the Holy Spirit to permeate your mind and heart and transform your thinking and feelings to align with His truth and make His truth a reality in your life.

From this moment forward, you are free to experience life as the chosen, set-apart, favored, beloved child of the Creator of the Universe that you truly are. Step into your true identity and begin to live out of it instead of striving to earn it. It's time to crossover from struggle and surviving to thriving in His land of promise and purpose.

CHAPTER NINE

Undoing

"I see how hard you work and all your exhausting efforts;
also your unyielding commitment to the task and how you
cannot stand the wicked ... You have applied great diligence
and have relentlessly pushed yourself beyond limits – and
all along you did it in my name, as if you were representing
me! Here is my problem, you have divorced me
and abandoned your first love."

—Revelation 2:2-4 *(THE MIRROR)*

THE TRUTHS BRIDGETT AND I EXPLORED were life chang-
ing, and their revelation intensified my desire to experience more of
God's power and presence. The more I pursued His heart, the greater
clarity I had. Some of the most transformative discoveries I made during
this period of my life was what I learned by drawing close to the Lord.

I know it's paradoxical, but though I helped my clients experience
His love and presence, I never felt it for myself. It seemed it was for
everybody else, but not for me.

I was tired of believing in who I'd always thought He was, what had been taught to me by the church and religion. I had learned *about* Him all my life. I was ready to trade intellectual understanding for a personal relationship.

Over the next few years, I pressed into God. I spent hours in His Word, reading and studying the scriptures, and immersing myself in His Presence. I listened to numerous pastors and Bible teachers. I studied everything I could about God's true character and nature, how to know and hear from Him, and how to access the victorious life He promised me.

I realized that religion plus my programming and society's success strategies interfered with my ability to connect with God. Gradually, He replaced my head knowledge with heart experience as I surrendered more to Him, exchanging my discipline, self-sufficiency, and performance for deep, authentic connection. I learned to trust and abide in Him.

One by one, I examined my expectations of myself and the things I thought I was supposed to do while inviting God into every decision, every thought, every idea. I unlearned much of what I thought I knew. I stepped off the crazy train of performance and busyness and walked into the arms of my heavenly Father.

This was my time of undoing.

FROM RELIGION TO RELATIONSHIP

For almost forty years, I had learned about the importance of reverence and right and wrong. I spent as much time in "church" as any good Southern Baptist ever has. I was well aware of what I should and shouldn't do to perform for God's approval. Most of what I learned was legalities. "Do this!" and "Don't do that." "Be like Jesus." I knew all about Him, but I didn't really know Him.

One of my favorite Bible teachers, Mike Parsons, talks about how religion actually inoculates us from experiencing God. My painful disappointments exacerbated my doctrinal misconceptions, resulting in me believing lies about God. He seemed like an absent father, a punisher, yet another "person" who loved me based on my performance. I thought I had to be good and do everything right to please Him and receive His blessing. "Holiness," as I understood it, derived from self-control and performance.

When we don't know who God really is and don't have an intimate personal relationship with Him, we have a distorted view of ourselves and life. It's crucial to learn who He is so that we can deconstruct all the lies we have believed. I set aside what I thought I knew about Him and decided to get to know Him intimately and personally.

I knew that I couldn't fix my problems with the same thinking that created them in the first place. I needed a new heart to understand and new eyes–spiritual eyes–to see a breakthrough in my life. What I needed was supernatural transformation.

When we live in self-sufficiency, lack, fear, and performance, we try to do enough and have enough to be good enough. We strive for God's blessing, but we miss His love. We misunderstand our true identity. We live like orphans and slaves, like outsiders, instead of sons and daughters who are heirs to a kingdom.

Six important spiritual disciplines helped me cultivate the deep and authentic relationship with God that I craved. As I replaced the lies I believed with truth, I discovered how to know my heavenly Father, how to experience Him, and how to hear His voice. Knowing Him intimately taught me how to break free from powerful strongholds so that I was free to live out my destiny. I also uncovered lies I had believed about myself, something we will talk about more as my story progresses.

I've incorporated these disciplines for many years now, walking with Him in a continually unfolding process that grows and deepens with time and experience. These habits were the foundation of my healing and maturing spiritually and are a guide for my steps to this day. I share them with you with the hope that they will lead you deeper into His heart and into the life of freedom and fullness that is awaiting you!

1. MEDITATE ON HIS WORD

Spending time in God's Word is key to understanding His nature, our identity in Him, and the life He promises us. We are powerful, divine beings, children of the King, so we are opposed by evil whose intent is to steal, kill, and destroy everything good God intended for us, including our trust in and connection with God Himself. In every moment, there is a battle for our hearts and minds. Our negative experiences cause us to believe lies about ourselves, God, and what is available to us. As a result, evil robs us of our true identity and inheritance and causes us to settle for a much smaller and harder existence than the life of abundance and victory God offers us.

The good news is that God is ready to rescue us. In Ephesians, Paul teaches:

"Put on God's complete set of armor provided for us, so that you will be protected as you fight against the evil strategies of the accuser. Your hand to hand combat is not with human beings, but with the highest principalities and authorities operating in rebellion in under the heavenly realms. For they are a powerful class of demon gods and evil spirits that hold this dark world in bondage. Because of this, you must wear all the armor that God provides so you're protected as you confront the slanderer, for you are destined for all things and will rise victorious. Put on truth as a belt to strengthen you to stand in triumph. Put on holiness as the protective armor that covers your heart. Stand on your feet alert and, then you'll always be ready to share the blessings of peace. In every battle, take faith as your wrap-around shield, for it is able to extinguish the blazing arrows coming at you from the Evil One! Embrace the power of salvation's full deliverance, like a helmet to protect your thoughts from lies. And take the mighty razor-sharp Spirit sword of the spoken word of God." —Ephesians 6:10-18 *(TPT)*

Paul refers to the word of God as the belt of truth and the Spirit sword as crucial pieces of armor that empower us to live victoriously over our enemy's attacks. Jesus was our greatest model for trusting and abiding daily with God. He demonstrated how we can live a life of freedom, victory, and purpose. Jesus knew the Word, spoke the Word, and applied the Word in all that He did. I deeply desired to have the kind of faith that Jesus did, living in the rest and trust in God, and I knew that reading, studying, and meditating on God's word was the way.

I was riveted by the Israelites' story, their journey from slavery to the Promised Land in the Old Testament. I read about their ongoing struggles throughout hundreds of years with so many of their own internal and external bondages. I related to their frustration (and to their self-pity and complaining). They had been enslaved by Pharaoh in Egypt for four hundred years before God supernaturally rescued them. Yet, after their rescue, they wandered in the wilderness for forty more years before finally reaching the Promised Land. They were God's chosen people, and He had personally guided them through Moses' leadership for the entire journey. What should have been a two-week trip to the land of freedom and abundance became four decades of wandering in struggle and survival because of their fear, doubt, and unbelief.

As the years passed, new generations emerged, and Joshua was called into leadership upon Moses' death. When God knew that the new generation of Israelite people was finally ready to enter into the land He had promised them, He charged Joshua, who had been Moses' assistant. He said:

"Get going. Cross this Jordan River, you and all the people. Cross to the country I'm giving to the people of Israel. I'm giving you every square inch of the land you set your foot on – just as I promised Moses. ... It's all yours. All your life, no one will be able to hold out against you. In the same way I was with Moses, I'll be with you. I won't give up on you. I won't leave you. Strength! Courage! You are going to lead this people to inherit the land that I promised to give their ancestors. Give it everything you have, heart and soul." —Joshua 1:2-6 *(The Message)*

Following His charge to Joshua to lead His people into the Promised Land, God commanded him to do three things to make his way successful.

"Keep this Book of the Law always on your lips; meditate on it day and night, so that you may be careful to do everything written in it. Then you will be prosperous and successful." —Joshua 1:8 (NIV)

After hundreds of years of struggle, these three simple commands brought huge breakthrough to the Israelite people. As I read those words, I knew there was transformative power in them.

I began to understand how important it is for me to immerse my heart and mind in His word on a daily basis so His truth could permeate my being, build up my spirit, and spark supernatural faith and courage in me. I knew that it would empower me to cross over from the land of struggle and bondage into the land of promise and purpose. We all need truth in the center of our being, grounding our foundation, connecting us to the heart of God, and setting us free from the devil's strongholds. We must press in deeply to God's word, seek a deep understanding of it, and meditate on it until it transforms our thinking and feeling.

Over the next days, weeks, months, and years, I searched God's word for wisdom and truth, which He generously revealed to me. You'll see how the breadth and power of His revelation continue to unfold in my story.

2. STUDY HIS CHARACTER

Before I could replace the lies I believed about God, I had to know His true character and nature. In my angry letter to God, it was evident that I didn't trust Him. To me, He was judgmental, punitive, absent, hard to please, demanding perfection, critical, and distant. I felt punished by Him. I had heard that God is love, and He is good and trustworthy, but that wasn't what I ever felt or experienced in my life. I only saw that He was all of those things to other people. He had left me out of His blessing. I didn't feel like His daughter at all. I felt lost–like an orphan–on my own.

One day in my time with God, I asked Him to reveal who He really is because I didn't want to serve a God like the one I pictured. I was done with that. I confided my true feelings to a dear friend who asked me a powerful question: "What do you think is so flawed and bad about you that God doesn't love you? What do you do so wrong that left you out of God's favor and blessing?"

Her response shifted something deep inside of me. I didn't have a good answer. So, I began to have hope that maybe I wasn't left out, but there was definitely something blocking me from knowing Him and receiving His love.

Over the next several years, I studied and listened to teachings on the character and nature of God, replacing the lies I had believed about Him with the truth of who He says He is. Fortunately, He wants to reveal the mysteries of Himself to us.

Another of my favorite Bible teachers, Graham Cooke, says, "What you think about God is the most important thought you will ever have...."

His blogs helped transform my view of God greatly. The way he describes God's heart towards His children is vastly different than what my religious upbringing taught me. Mr. Cooke focuses on God as deeply loving, gracious, and tender.

"He is relentlessly loving and kind, and He will never quit on you," Mr. Cooke says. That's a very different perspective than an absent father or a harsh judge, which is what I had grown up believing.

The more I discovered, the more I wanted to know and understand more. One morning as I was studying God's word, He led me to Isaiah, where He expresses His deep love for us as His children.

"I want them back, every last one who bears my name, every man, woman, and child whom I created for my glory, yes, personally formed and made each one." —Isaiah 43:7 *(The Message)*

"That includes you," I heard Him speak into my Spirit. Then, I was led to Isaiah, where He says:

"I'd sell off the whole world to get you back, trade the creation just for you." —Isaiah 43:4 *(The Message)*

Again, I heard Him say, "Yes, you."

There are so many more beautiful descriptors of God's character and nature revealed to us in the Bible. He is our Shepherd, Father, Healer, Provider, Friend, the Lover of our Soul, Guide, Protector, and the Great Warrior, among many others. Shifting my perspective about His true nature and character deepened my desire to spend time getting to know Him personally.

3. SPEND TIME IN HIS PRESENCE

It is impossible to experience and connect with Him with only our intellect. It became clear to me that God desires us to know Him, to really KNOW Him, and to connect with us spirit to Spirit. We can only find Him when we seek Him with our whole heart.

Initially, my programming interfered with my ability to experience God. My schedule was full of all the things I was striving to achieve, all of the structure and discipline required to accomplish my goals. Even the "quiet time" I set aside to spend with the Lord was a structure of readings and prayers. I was not experiencing God because I was slave-driving myself through every minute of my life. I realized that "doing" was my problem, especially when I was "doing" outside of Him.

The stress in my life had to be quieted. I had to settle myself, find the quiet place where I could hear Him. This discipline takes practice. We are so accustomed to anesthetizing ourselves with the distractions of our world—commitments, activities, work, chores—we don't realize how clamorous our lives become. He's not in the noise and chaos. He's in the stillness.

I found my quiet place in nature, where I can take a deep breath and be present. I spent more time in the places where my heart was most connected, most fully alive—in nature, with animals, praise music, running—whatever brought my heart life. As I pressed into God, I began setting aside just an hour of unstructured time each day, inviting Him into whatever I was doing that was playful, creative, or enjoyable for me, and He began showing up. As I engaged His heart, he began to transform my mind, deconstructing religion and legality, and He became real. I wanted to know God personally. I wanted the transformation that only He can do inside of me and in my life.

It turns out, He wants to co-create with us! He wants to walk with us in the garden in the cool of the day as He did with Adam. He speaks to us in quiet times, in nature, play, and creativity. I learned that He's not a slave driver! Instead, when we spend time with Him, He confirms who we are, how He loves us, what He has for us. He wants to enjoy us!

I began to understand that worship is spending time in His presence. I read and listened to sermons about how the power of praise and worship empowers the reality of heaven to manifest on earth. I would worship many days until the atmosphere changed, and I would soak in the Presence of God. I would listen to praise and worship music while lying down or sitting or walking in nature, where I took my focus off of myself and my circumstances and shifted them onto God. Then I would experience the power and peace of His presence.

Powerful shifts happen when we see God, ourselves, and life differently. New eyes allow us to see His truth. When we expand our awareness beyond what we've experienced in the past, when we see something else, something new, we can feel hope. There is light in the darkness. Possibilities exist where they didn't before!

Now I understand that God is concerned with our holiness, but we don't earn it the way I thought we did. It's not about what we do or don't do. Instead, it's about how much we understand and comprehend. We can't be holy until we know His love. When we encounter Him, when His love for us permeates us, we respond to being loved. Our relationship changes from seeing God as an acquaintance, someone we know or know about to knowing Him as our friend.

When we really meet and encounter Him, when we are in a relationship with Him, then we are transformed, and so is our life. His Holy Spirit performs heart surgery on us because of who He is and how He loves us. *This* is what makes us holy. His holiness is expressed in us.

4. ALIGN WITH HIS SPIRIT

The Holy Spirit takes up residence in us when we are saved and empowers us to overcome sin and live for God's glory and purpose. This is the same powerful Spirit that empowered Jesus and the disciples to live in connection with God, overcome temptation, fulfill their anointing, and perform miracles. It is literally the power of God in us. When we receive the Holy Spirit, He begins a work in us to transform us into the image of Christ. The same power that guided Jesus' every movement on earth is available to lead, convict, teach, and equip us to do God's work.

We can choose to feed and strengthen the Spirit in us or ignore it. We can live distracted, on our own in our own knowledge and strength, or we can allow the Holy Spirit to enable us to exchange a flesh-driven existence to one led by God. I chose to embrace His Spirit in another critical step to drawing closer to God.

My desire now is to live so in tune with the Holy Spirit that I do nothing outside of what He's doing and who He created me to be. I spent years striving, struggling, and surviving in my own strength, and knowledge and ability. It's an exhausting life that leads only to weariness and burnout. It's not fruitful.

We are created and intended to walk in the Spirit. In Galatians 5, scripture tells us to "live life in the continual presence of God." What does this look like? It's a God-consciousness all day, every day. We talk to Him about everything. As we align with the Holy Spirit, it transforms us from the inside out–creates new desires, yearnings, and longings inside of us. Every decision and action is guided either by the Holy Spirit or our flesh. When we walk in the Spirit, we live on a higher level where victory reigns and righteousness rules.

To walk in the Spirit is to live a new life in Jesus Christ. We walk away from a life of bondage into the free and full life where His Spirit is the ruling and governing principle in our life, always speaking to and guiding us. We live life in all its details, from am to pm, by the power of the Holy Spirit.

"But when the Father sends the Spirit of Holiness, the One like me who sets you free, he will teach you all things in my name." —John 14:26 *(TPT)*

When we are hungry to know and engage with God's heart and spend time and energy doing that, we release those things that enslave us. We feed the Spirit in us and starve the flesh.

The way of the Spirit is a path of surrender which leads to a fullness of life. The Holy Spirit guides the way and empowers us. We learn to align with His Spirit, His harmony, His flow, His unforced rhythms of grace.

Obeying Him is impossible for our flesh and in our strength. It's a shift we make in our minds and hearts. We begin by practicing being still, quieting our minds, minimizing distractions and self-sufficiency, and releasing our do-it-yourself mindset and habits.

If we seek to maintain an awareness of the Holy Spirit's presence and are sensitive to Him, He gives us sensitivity to the things of God and understanding about our situations in life and how to proceed.

There's a difference in having knowledge and revelatory wisdom. When we spend time connecting in alignment with Him, we can receive His revelatory wisdom. He wants to reveal the mysteries of Himself to us. He wants to tell us how He sees us, how He feels about us, and who we are supernaturally. He wants to show us what piece of His heart we have that is uniquely ours.

When we live spirit to Spirit–in constant communication with Him–we can hear His voice in our spirit. How do I "hear" his voice? He speaks into my spirit. Sometimes things just come to me. It sounds like my own voice, but it's calm, peaceful, nurturing. I've learned how to know it's Him. His voice is loving, grace-filled, sometimes even playful.

Hearing His voice and how He sees and loves us, knowing how He designed us, reveals who we are and whose we are. We learn to walk in our purpose, fueled by passion, as opposed to being driven.

Hearing from God is life-changing. Consider how Jesus lived. He regularly went off to be alone with His Father. He prayed in gardens. He sought seclusion in the desert. Jesus lived from the overflow of the time spent with His Father. As a result, He answered the call of God's heart. Jesus didn't meet every need. Instead, He waited for instructions and favor from His Father. Allowing God to help us make decisions, asking Him what to do and what not to do, produces fruit. Acting otherwise, at best, is counterproductive and exhausting. At worst, we can lose our way in every way you can imagine.

When we hear from God, we begin to understand who He is. Only then can we see that we are His children, each of us uniquely designed with gifts, strengths, and passions. Even our idiosyncrasies, the little things about us that make us who we are, are given to us for a reason. We have a part to play in a bigger story that He's writing, and what a beautiful and powerful story it is!

5. COMMUNICATE WITH GOD

What is our role in His bigger story? Our Heavenly Father wants to tell us! He wants us to know specifically who we are, how He created us, and how He loves us uniquely. When we press into Him, He will reveal our identity, our purpose, and the destiny He designed us for. We simply have to ask Him.

We must be willing to ask Him the hard questions, the confusing questions, the "dumb" questions – *all* of our questions. I ask Him all kinds of questions, and I just keep asking until He gives me answers. I have an open dialog with Him all day. I ask Him what to do in any and every situation.

I have asked Him all kinds of things like, "Who are You?" "How did You create me?" "How do You see me?" "What did You create me for?" "What did You make so special about me?"

One day, as I spent time with Him in the stillness of nature, He said to me, "You are the beauty of My heart. You see My beauty all around, and you're a reflection of the beauty of My heart to others."

This was so special to me. I realized this is not about my physical appearance. Rather, it is about my appreciation of beauty in the world. I see beauty in people. I see beauty in animals. I stop and notice the beauty around me every day because He created me to appreciate aesthetics. It's a gift He's given me.

"I just want you to notice the beauty and share that with the world," God told me. "I want you to know the beauty of My heart and share that with people."

What a transforming revelation! My religion told me to do, do, do, and then do some more. God told me to slow down and notice the beauty around me. When we abide and trust in Him every day, He loves to honor our faith in action when we do what He says.

Satan specializes in twisting our God-given gifts. Before I understood my gift, I almost hated myself. My love of beauty, distorted, became an eating disorder and an obsession with my appearance. I had to wear a certain kind of clothes. My body had to look a certain way. I went overboard, spending money on beautiful things and binging on sugary and fatty foods because my creativity was stifled. God showed me how that gift was meant for good.

Our gift, our purpose, the thing God put in us is the thing Satan uses against us to prevent us from living out our destiny. When we believe the enemy's lies about us, he twists our gift and steals our destiny. He will do anything to thwart our purpose because he fears that if we discover it and get free, we will be on fire in our anointing and unstoppable for the Kingdom.

We live victoriously over the enemy's evil schemes by staying in constant communion with God. Religion often leads us to believe that God is in a far-away Heaven, but scripture tells us that we are God's residence. His "Spirit" actually means "breath" in Hebrew, so we can rest assured that God is as close as the air that we breathe. We don't have to chase after Him, but simply "tune in" to His Spirit within us.

As uniquely as He has wired each of us, this is how distinctively He wants to speak to us. He wants to reveal truth to us in a way that we will hear and understand. Even when we read scripture, He wants to speak His word afresh to our specific situation and offer us revelatory wisdom for every season in our life.

Turn to Him all day, every day, like we would a friend. Stop and ask Him for direction, then follow His way. When we ask His input in every decision, we hear what His heart is. He shows us how to spend our time and energy. As a result, we live in His flow, His favor, and His abundance to fulfill our purpose.

6. REST

When we immerse ourselves in His Presence and His Word, we are changed. We discover the most beautiful gift He's given us: complete and utter dependence on Him for everything we need. This feels scary, even weird. It doesn't make sense to us, but it's how He calls us to live, and it's how He sets us free. We are not called to strive, struggle, and survive. We're called to thrive and, paradoxically, to rest and abide in Him.

Once again, consider Jesus as our model for living. He did things that God put in His heart or spoke to Him about specifically. He didn't do things out of performance or need. He knew who the Father was, and He knew how much He was loved. Jesus understood His inheritance and knew that He was always going to have everything He needed in abundance to complete the work that God had given Him to do. He didn't try to run in somebody else's lane or do work that wasn't His. He didn't try to please people or seek approval. He lived by passion, compassion, the gifts that God had given Him, not by a drivenness or out of need.

He rested. He wasn't caught up in the world's way. He listened to everything the Father said to Him and did what the Father said and did. He didn't do anything because He had to make a living. He knew that God always provided everything He needed. He asked the Father for what He needed. He spoke the truth of the Word of God. He lived in wholeness and harmony with God's Spirit. He slept in storms. He didn't hurry. Even when pressed by those closest to Him, He was steady because the Father does everything from a place of rest.

When we understand who we are in Him, we don't have to be somebody else or do what other people expect us to do. We live from our Power Source, centered in the mold He created for us. This is so foreign to us, counter-intuitive and counter-cultural, but I understand it more and more. God promised the Israelites they would live in the land of milk and honey. It wasn't about wealth and riches and having stuff. He wanted them to rest in who He had made them to be, to live in the abundance that overflows from living as sons and daughters. He promised peace and rest in this new land, but their unbelief and inability to listen left them stuck in the wilderness.

The fourth chapter of Hebrews talks about their journey and about rest.

"For as long, then, as that promise of resting in Him pulls us on to God's goal for us, we need to be careful that we're not disqualified. We received the same promises as those people in the wilderness, but the promises didn't do them a bit of good because they didn't receive the promises with faith. If we believe, though, we'll experience that state of resting. But not if we don't have faith. Remember that God said, Exasperated, I vowed, "They'll never get where they're going, never be able to sit down and rest." —Hebrews 4:1-3 *(The Message)*

I knew this passage was for me. But once again, my programming and discipline were in the way. I had to stop performing and quit doing some things, even "good" things. I let go of anything that felt heavy. Anything that felt hard or forceful, I stopped doing, even when it didn't make sense. I started asking God about each move I made, how I spent my time, energy, and resources in every moment. I learned to let Him keep me aligned with my purpose by showing me the difference between what's good and what's best. I asked Him about every client I saw, everything I wrote, and everything I took on.

I began to take a Sabbath rest. I gave Him time to refuel and recharge me. The result was much more peace and fulfillment and clarity about what was important. And guess what: I got much more done.

God wants us to connect with Him, to live out of His Spirit in us. To do that, we have to learn how to be still, quiet ourselves, and connect to our hearts. He breathes life into us when we rest. Striving and forcing things drains us dry. When we live in fear or need, our world gets so small, like we have blinders on. When we live close-fisted, in tight control, we become isolated, compressed, diminished. But when we live from a place of rest and utter dependence on the Lord, He shows us all kinds of things we can't see on our own. He fills our vessel. The whole world opens up for us when we live open and willing to receive from Him.

My undoing was actually the key to my freedom. My surrender–the white flag raised when I finally said, "I can't do this anymore"–led me into the rescuing arms of Jesus. As I soaked in His wisdom and truth and learned His ways, I began to transform from the inside out. I persevered in these daily disciplines, and over time, they became my new way of living. God began to close the gap between my head and my heart, bringing together what I knew and what I felt. As I absorbed His presence and the truth of His word, my life changed, too. Ultimately, the shift has been so profound, that I want nothing more than to help others experience the freedom and fulfillment I have.

Because of my struggles, I recognize when others face similar obstacles. My experiences equipped me to see the traps so many of us commonly fall into. While the Lord was showing me how to climb up from a bottom of despair, He also gave me insight into how to help others rise up and walk in their destiny, too. If you've ever felt your hopes and dreams were smothered by reality, stay with me for a resurrecting remedy.

REFLECTION

*"You will seek me and find me when you seek
me with all your heart."*

—Jeremiah 29:13 *(ESV)*

How has your religious upbringing affected the way you view God? What do you believe about God as a result?

How have your disappointments influenced your beliefs about who God is?

Do you find yourself performing for God's approval and blessing but missing His love? What does that look like? How does this affect your relationship with Him?

What is the desire of your heart for your relationship with God?

What is preventing you from experiencing intimacy with God? (Busyness? Distractions? Stress? Noise? Intellect?) Be specific.

What are you doing out of your self-sufficiency or drivenness that leaves you overwhelmed, exhausted, frustrated, or burned out?

What would it look like for you to live Holy Spirit-led versus being task driven? If you lived life from a place of rest and trust in God instead of striving, struggling, surviving, how differently would life look and feel? What would change for you?

In what area(s) of your life do you need a breakthrough? What supernatural transformation do you need to happen?

APPLICATION

"Snuggle up to the warm embrace of God;
experience His closeness."

—James 4:8 *(THE MIRROR)*

Tell God what the desire of your heart is for a relationship with Him.

Ask Him your deepest questions. What do you really want to know His truth about? Who He is? Who you are? Why He created you? What does He want to create with you? Ask Him. Study His word for answers.

Spend time quieting yourself in His presence. Engage His heart. Go where you connect most to your heart and where you feel fully alive. Invite Him into that space with you. Open your heart and receive His goodness and love.

Ask Him to make Himself real and to reveal His wisdom to you. Go deeper. Seek Him until He shows you or until you hear His voice. Then, keep pressing in. As you spend time with Him, He will confirm who He is, who you are, how He loves you, and what He has for you.

He wants to enjoy you, to fill you with His Spirit, and overwhelm you with His love. Open your heart to Him and commit to getting to know Him as your friend. As you do, He will transform your heart, mind, and your life!

CHAPTER TEN

Buried Alive

"This is the message of light: Christ awakens you from your
intoxicated slumber and resurrects you out of the
death trap of enslaved thought patterns."

—Ephesians 5:14 *(THE MIRROR)*

AS I CONTINUED TO FERVENTLY SEEK the Lord, His power and presence transformed me. Lies I had believed for most of my life began to unravel. My enemy aimed to neutralize my impact and influence, but God deflected this arrow with truth. I saw how all along He fought for my heart against the darkness that pursued it.

He gave me a family that loved me the best way they knew how. They instilled a profound desire in me to help others and when I struggled, they sheltered me. He sent Angel to teach me how to take care of the little girl inside and to send my protector self into retirement. When I surrendered a counterfeit identity rooted in performance, He snuggled me in a robe of righteousness and seated me at the family table as a beloved daughter.

The more I marveled at how He intervened on my behalf, the more I understood that He doesn't want us to settle for merely managing our pain. He wants us to break free from the lies and shame, to be truly healed and whole. He longs to replace defeat and discouragement with freedom and fullness, to turn discouragement into victory, and to lead us to a destiny that fulfills His will and our purpose.

He showed me that performance is not the answer. He wants to be the source of everything I do, every day. He wants me to have what I need in order to be completely free, and to equip me to set people free in the work that I do.

There was still more He wanted to show me. In a powerful moment of revelation, He revealed to me how we can break free from the lies and shame that enslave us once and for all.

PRISON OF DARKNESS

It happened one day in an inner healing prayer session with one of my clients, when God reminded her of a very painful event in her childhood. As she recalled the details and relived the scene, He showed her a deep lie that she believed as a result. This lie had distorted and stolen so much of her true identity and the life He intended for her.

Satan had used that circumstance to whisper a lie to her, and it had kept her imprisoned in the bondage of self-hatred, self-sabotage, and sex and drug addiction for more than twenty-five years. Just like that, though, in our session God's Presence shined His light of truth on that lie, and my client's heart began to heal. As He spoke her true identity to her, she was freed from that prison of darkness. He showed her how He was redeeming the pain from the event in her life, transforming what evil had meant for bad into something He would use for good.

On that day, the Holy Spirit downloaded to me a clear picture of how the enemy preys on, enslaves, and steals from us. He also showed me the path to our healing and freedom. Since then, God has unveiled more wisdom on the entire process of our emotional wounding and the far-reaching effects it has on us, along with the coping mechanisms, defenses, and manifestations that we experience as a result. This truth led to a powerfully transformative healing process that freed me and hundreds of my clients who have walked it out with me. If you crave wholeness, freedom, and the fullness of life God offers us, this is for you.

I have shared how we are born behind enemy lines into a world of pain and brokenness. From early in our childhood and as we grow and develop, we build our perspective of ourselves and of life on a foundation of lies we receive through negative messages from people and experiences. Conveyed to us verbally and nonverbally, directly and indirectly, often by people we love, respect, and admire most, these messages become like arrows that deeply wound our hearts and spirits.

These arrows tell us we are flawed, worthless, different, even dark and twisted. They say things like, "If you ever let anyone see that part of you, then they're not going to accept or approve of you." "If you ever let anybody know that you feel that way, it will upset them, and they won't like you." "You'd better hide that part of you from others because they're going to think you're weird."

"You're dumb for feeling like that, or for wanting or liking that." "You don't fit in." "You're too much—too fat, too dumb, too slow, too messy, too short, too tall, too boring, etc." "You're not enough—not cool enough, not pretty enough, not skinny enough, not athletic enough, not rich enough, not smart enough, not fun enough, etc."

The lies we come to believe about ourselves vary for each of us, but they are similar in theme. They say "You're not significant or important." "You don't have what it takes." "You're not lovable or acceptable." "You don't matter."

As a result, we feel that we are less than, sub-par. Shame accompanies the lies and condemns us. "You're the problem." "You're all alone." "You're the only one who hasn't done it right." "You're the only one who feels this way."

These aspects of us feel inadequate and detestable. Then, our survival nature decides that we will do whatever we have to do to conceal our inadequacies. Whether consciously, subconsciously, or unconsciously, we lock away those unacceptable, defective parts of ourselves never to be exposed again. We bury them underground, and we close off places in our hearts, believing our hearts can never be trusted again.

HAUNTED

Once we have buried the shameful, inadequate parts of ourselves deeply underground, we create what I call a "false self," a version of ourselves that we believe will be acceptable and likable to others. At this point, the lies have convinced us that "If I want to be loved, accepted, and approved of, I need to look, feel, think, or act differently than I do."

Because we crave acceptance and belonging, we compare ourselves to others who seem to be popular, acceptable, or to have what it takes. We work hard to fill the ache we feel inside with things we hope will redeem the authentic parts we've hidden.

We overcompensate for our inadequacies by capitalizing on what we are good at so that we may become "somebody." We seek our identity and our value in achievement, performance, education, grades, love, relationships, attention, fame, popularity, success, money, humor, beauty, sports, sex, drugs, alcohol, food, fun–whatever makes us feel good. We focus on whatever makes us feel whole, complete, and loved.

Yet, no matter how hard we try to feel the way we want to feel or get the attention and approval we want and need, we are continuously haunted by the lies that we believe about ourselves. Those messages we have received continually tell us that we don't have what it takes, that we are never enough, and that we are not lovable or acceptable as we are. We can never do enough or be enough to make up for our flaws and inadequacies.

To quiet the lies in our minds and hearts, we bury these parts of ourselves even deeper. We call in reinforcements to suppress these aspects of ourselves that we've deemed inadequate and unacceptable. We form an alter ego, a protector self, whose job is to make sure that the shameful, "less than par" aspects of ourselves never resurface.

We align with this protector self, and it becomes an ally who likes to call the shots. We depend on him or her to motivate and discipline us to achieve and perform.

Remember Strong Connie, my alter ego, my protector self? She constantly berated me in my mind, saying things like, "you better not ever," "you cannot," "you've got to keep doing this," "If you ever let people see the real you," she would say, "your inadequacies will be exposed."

Eventually, we shut down our heart and hand over control of our mind and will to this alter ego, and it takes the reigns, along with control of our life.

Our fierce inner critic admonishes us constantly to be better, achieve more, never let anyone see our vulnerability. He or she is a counterfeit warrior who builds walls to prevent the things we bury from being exposed. As we hand over more power and control to our protector self, he or she torments us, stealing life, peace, and happiness. They become the superintendent of the graveyard where we've buried our shame. Their whole objective is to keep our inadequacies underground.

RESURRECTING THE HEART

I'm so grateful that God has provided several incredibly anointed counselors, coaches, and spiritual mentors to shepherd my heart. Neither scars nor healing happens overnight. My ongoing journey to healing and freedom has spanned almost thirty years. Though it felt like punishment at the time, I now recognize that I was blessed to start my healing journey in my twenties, earlier than most.

My wounds were deep, and the lies entrenched. My ego constructed Strong Connie to help me survive. She empowered me to struggle and strive my way to significant levels of achievement and success in life. But it came at a great cost to my heart, my relationships, and my enjoyment of life. The barricade I had built to protect me from the deep sense of inadequacy and unworthiness has taken many years of therapy and coaching to tear down. The walls that imprisoned me did not come down gently or quickly.

One Christmas, while visiting with my parents, my brother, Philly, and his new wife, Denise, I shared some of my pain and disappointment about where I was in life. Both Philly and Denise had worked with a Christian counselor, separately and together, in Tennessee. Ken had helped my brother heal from a painful divorce. Philly experienced so much freedom and healing, breaking free from some of his own performance mindset, that he loves to introduce Ken to others seeking the same. My brother offered to gift me a year of working with Ken biweekly.

I was so excited and grateful to have this opportunity, we got started right away. I began talking to him by phone mostly but drove up for a few extended sessions throughout the year. Ken's familiarity with our family dynamic fast-forwarded the process for me.

I'll never forget what Ken said to me during one of our first in-person sessions in his office and how healing it was to my soul. I don't remember much that led to it, except that I was sharing with him the pressure and the sadness I had felt growing up in my family. I told him how grateful I was to have experienced so much healing from working with my therapist, Angel, but I knew there was more that kept me in bondage that I needed to unlock.

I shared with Ken how I had viewed and treated myself because of the lies I had believed about me. Though I felt no longer wounded by those experiences, I still struggled sometimes with fear, shame, and self-doubt. I explained that though I knew the lies weren't true, and I no longer felt the intensity of their sting, they still whispered to me in some vulnerable moments. I poured my heart out about the sadness I still felt about the disappointment and loss I had experienced for so many years.

As I shared my heart, Ken connected with me–he totally got it. When I finished pouring out my pain, he slid to the front of his big leather chair, leaned in towards me, and spoke with compassion and sincerity.

"You know, Connie, it's like you've been buried alive your whole life," he said. "Nobody knew what to do with you, so they forced you into who they needed you to be."

My mom was the oldest of two children. Her father, a Navy officer, was an abusive alcoholic. Ken explained that her dad may have made her uncomfortable with her femininity. He also noted that with my dad being gone so much, she was forced to play a man's role in many ways as head of the household in her marriage. Plus, men and football were worshipped in my family.

"As a result, you weren't welcomed, celebrated, or nurtured as the little girl that you were then, or as the woman you have become," he said.

He pointed out that to Philly, I was irritating and in the way because he felt he had to perform, to be man enough in a male-dominated, athletic world, while also filling the role of Mom's emotional partner in my dad's absence. It was damaging and overwhelming to him in many ways, too. And in his pain, he wounded me.

"There was no room for your heart or your needs in that environment," Ken said. "You learned quickly to man up, to perform–to be strong and armored. And you survived, Connie."

It even worked well for me for a while, Ken noted. The tragedy in all of that was that the real Connie–little girl Connie–was buried alive.

"And you've done everything you can to keep her there," he said.

The truth of his words hit me at my core. Everything finally made sense. Every day of my life had been about keeping that little girl inside of me, the one who wasn't enough, hidden and locked underground. I believed I had to be my own hero. There was no other way to prove my value and earn an identity for myself.

Ken's words had summed up all of the pain I had experienced for so many years. I felt seen, known, and understood like I never had before by another person–especially by a man–which was incredibly healing for me. Finally, I could really see, know, and understand myself like never before. I felt a deep love and affection with my little girl, the real me that had been buried underground for all of those years.

"What I see you doing now is digging in the dirt, digging yourself out of that old grave, and unearthing the real you," Ken said. "You're coming back to life. You're discovering and embracing your femininity, your softness, your beauty, and your worthiness. I see you, Connie. I see your little girl, and I see the incredible woman that you are, and she is good. She is lovable. She is valuable, and she is enough."

The gift that Ken gave me in that session is priceless, and I will forever be grateful to him for those healing words. What an incredibly healing experience that he saw me. He SAW ME. He got me at every level because our hearts are so much alike. Being seen, known, and understood by a man in a healthy way–a man who didn't need or want anything from me, a man who didn't need me to perform, and one who was completely gracious, loving, and accepting of me in every way was about the most incredible gift I could have received in that season of my life.

There is no gift like that of being seen, understood, and accepted for who we are. That is the incredible gift of counseling, and I'm grateful now that as a therapist, I have shared very similar moments with my clients when I see them for who they really are and help them unearth their true selves and come back to life.

Most of us are comfortable remaining in our disconnection, our self-sufficiency, our self-protection. We settle for struggling, striving, and surviving. Anesthetizing our pain and shame with our cheap imitations, we love our vices for the instant gratification and the relief they provide. But if we are honest with ourselves, we aren't satisfied with a counterfeit. In the quiet moments when we are alone, we yearn to be seen, to be truly known, and to feel fully accepted and loved for who we really are. We long for true connection and intimacy with those we love and with God Himself. We hunger for internal peace and deeper fulfillment in life.

It exists, and it is available to us. God placed the desire in our hearts, and He will fulfill it in us. But to access it, we have to be willing to do something different. We have to do the heart work to heal the emotional wounds and resulting lies, and to eradicate the shame. Then we can reconnect with our hearts and live authentically. Resurrection healing requires us to be open and ready to:

1. Go back for the parts of ourselves that we have buried underground.

2. Reconnect to our own heart and to the heart of God, allowing Him to reveal the truth about the lies we have believed and about the painful experiences that hold us in bondage.

3. Dethrone our Counterfeit Warrior, evicting the harsh, critical voice that incites shame, fear, and doubt.

Stay with me as we address these three steps to healing in the next chapter.

REFLECTION

*"He rescued us from the dominion of darkness and relocated us
into the Kingdom where the love of His son rules."*

—Colossians 1:13 (*THE MIRROR*)

What painful experiences and messages (arrows) have pierced your
heart? What lies have you come to believe about yourself as a result?
How have these lies stolen from you? What has been the result?

How does shame condemn you? What does it tell you about you?

What parts of yourself have you buried underground?

How have you overcompensated for your perceived inadequacies so
you can feel like somebody? Where have you sought your identity
and value?

How have you allied with your protector self? What does he/she tell
you that keeps you motivated, disciplined, and strong? How has that
worked for you? What has it cost you?

APPLICATION

"Your indifferent mindset alienated you from God into a lifestyle of annoyances, hardships, and labors. Yet He has now fully reconciled and restored you to your original design."

—Colossians 1:21 (THE MIRROR)

It's time to unearth the real you–all of you–that you shamed and buried underground long ago because you were given messages that you are not enough or too much, that you are not accepted, wanted, or loved for who you really are.

Spend time identifying the parts of you that you have hated and rejected for so long. Choose to see those parts of you through eyes of compassion, understanding, love, and acceptance.

It's time to bring you back to life and embrace yourself–imperfections and all–and begin to live healed and wholeheartedly as the just-right you that you really are!

Are you ready?

CHAPTER ELEVEN

Resurrection

"In this world you will have trouble. But take heart!
I have overcome the world."

—John 16:33 *(NIV)*

THE PROCESS OF INNER HEALING can feel scary and over-whelming. These feelings are merely schemes of the enemy to keep us trapped in the vicious cycle of lies and bondage. Continuing to live in our pain is what keeps us stuck.

No one, including me, wants to revisit our most painful experiences. We will do anything to avoid dealing with our deepest wounds. We don't want to acknowledge, much less make peace with, the parts of ourselves that we have deemed inadequate or sub-par. However, continuing to avoid those parts of us causes us more misery every day than we can even imagine or understand. Listening to and believing the voice of our harsh inner critic beats us down, diminishing who we really are and stealing from us the MORE that God has for us.

The truth is that it is way more uncomfortable to cope with the pain that colors everything we think, say, feel, and do than it is to go through the process of inner healing. Remaining wounded and heart-broken, settling for relieving our aches and pains through our vices, just moves us farther away from what we most deeply desire. It's past time to stop the vicious cycle of lies and deception and start living the life God intended for us.

Looking back, I am incredibly grateful that I reached the point in my life where none of my vices were working for me anymore. I was exhausted by trying to self-redeem my story with all the human effort I could muster. Only when I was at the very end of myself was I open to seeing anything other than the ineffective patterns of thinking and behaving that had kept me stuck in bondage for so many years. Until then, I could not see or understand God's truth because the enemy's lies so blinded me.

When I was ready, the revelation came. And now it is my privilege to share some of the most important steps in the journey to healing.

DISCOVER YOUR INNER CHILD

The first step of the journey to inner healing is to resurrect the parts of ourselves that we have buried underground. As long as we continue to believe that certain parts of us are shameful or flawed, keeping those aspects of ourselves hidden away, we won't be or feel worthy or be whole. We will remain injured, struggling to survive, or striving to feel like we are enough. We must go back for our true self, accepting and embracing him or her. We must realize that because someone else, in response to their own pain, gave us messages about our value and lovability doesn't mean that we have to accept those arrows as our truth.

The truth is this: God loves every piece of us. He created us to live wholeheartedly in the fullness of who He made us. Then, and only then, we can experience the completeness of His love, His blessings, and His destiny for us. We can't afford to stay wounded and broken. We must not settle for merely managing our lives by coping with our pain. We must decide to heal, to bring in our scattered, tattered, and simply human pieces, and finally accept and embrace who we really are–who God created us to be. He accepts us, and His description of us is that we are "good, very good."

Let's go a step further with this thought. Even if there is something we don't like about ourselves, we cannot begin to change it as long as we are burying it or avoiding it, shaming, blaming, and hating ourselves for it. This gives it even more power, making it a much bigger issue–a place of bondage, rather than a place we can let God into to transform.

When we received the wounding messages from others, each of us was an innocent child who was doing the very best we could with what we were given at the time. And our child was just that–merely a child–not bad, shameful, or inadequate. That inner child, our emotional, creative, playful self, is still with us. Our child is stuck, though, at the emotional age when he or she was wounded.

We must go back and rescue this child, allowing God to redeem his or her painful experience. Until we set our inner child free, fear, self-doubt, and shame will color everything we do. We will live half-hearted and half-asleep.

I would bet that you are much more critical than you are nurturing to your inner child–I know I was. We tend to parent in either a nurturing or a critical way, based upon the model set by our parents or parental figures. Stop and think about the emotional damage this constant criticism does to the most precious and innocent part of you. If you were to treat your own child like you treat your inner child, how would that affect him or her? How would he or she feel living with that criticism, ridicule, and abuse all day, every day? No one can thrive in that kind of environment. It would be emotionally and mentally damaging. Yet we expect ourselves to excel in spite of that kind of mistreatment. It's not possible! The punishment has to stop!

If we continue to shame that precious inner child and keep him or her buried, we are choosing abuse. Instead, we have to decide to go back for our child in the same place we buried them long ago. We must resurrect that child, embracing all the parts of us. We need to forgive ourselves for not knowing what we didn't know and learn to love ourselves for the special and unique creation that we are.

Even the parts of us that seem irritating or that we struggle with are there for a reason. For example, the things I hated most about myself–being non-productive, undisciplined, and messy–were criticized most by my mom and brother. Now I understand that being creative, free-spirited, intuitive, and empathic are some of my greatest gifts. Being intense or super disciplined hardens the edges of these gifts.

Similarly, certain qualities are essential for you to fulfill your unique calling. Some of the things we struggle with most are not flaws but simply areas for growth. As we partner with God as our heavenly Father, allowing Him to love, nurture, and guide us, we learn how to parent our inner child in a nurturing way. As we experience His unconditional love and acceptance, we begin to participate in the healing of our heart wounds. Then, and only then, can we begin to live freely, fully, and wholeheartedly in who He created us to be.

EMBRACE HIS TRUTH ABOUT YOU

God doesn't say we are good if we perform to a certain standard. He doesn't say we are beautiful if we look like that picture. He doesn't call us His Beloved only if we are smart enough, cool enough, or successful enough. Instead, He says that we are fearfully and wonderfully made (Psalm 139), that "I have called your name. You are mine...I paid a huge price for you...that's how much you mean to me! That's how much I love you! I'd sell off the whole world to get you back, trade the creation just for you." (Isaiah 43)

Ponder this: If the most perfect, majestic, and all-knowing being who created all of heaven and earth speaks that highly of us and loves us that much, then why don't we believe Him?

It's only because we have bought into the vicious lies of the evil one who used other people's pain and brokenness to communicate negative, hurtful messages to us about our worth and value.

It is time that we set ourselves free from the lies we have believed about ourselves. Maybe you got the message that you are too much or not enough from someone along the way in your life. Maybe that message has been reinforced over and over again to you through multiple people and experiences. That idea is nothing but a reflection of the pain of that person who gave you that message. It actually had nothing to do with you at all. It is NOT who you are.

To free yourself from the lie, you have to be willing to stop accusing and shaming yourself. By continuing to believe and reinforce it, you're fortifying the stronghold the devil has put in place in your mind and heart. But it is a LIE from the depths of HELL! It is NOT WHO YOU ARE! Say it with me out loud: that is not who God says I am, so that is not who I am.

I have taken hundreds of clients through the therapeutic process called Inner Child Healing, and I have experienced my own personal healing through this same technique. Through guided visualization in a deep, relaxed state, I encourage the client to visualize his or her inner child. Usually, they picture their child to be anywhere from four to eight years old, at an age when they were most innocent and most fully alive. I ask them to describe their features, their dress, and their personality. Every time, they describe themselves with such specificity.

It enables them to really connect with their inner child and visually bring him or her to life. It's amazing.

Once they picture and connect with their inner child, I ask them to recall a time or memory when they first felt the painful emotion or heard the words that keep them stuck and in pain today. If they don't connect to a specific memory, I ask them to remember a time when they felt sad, hurt, or alone. They can always remember a moment when they were hurt, shamed, mistreated, or rejected by someone, often a parent, sibling, friend, or sometimes an abuser. These scenarios are often the root of the lies they believe about themselves, their value, and lovability. In these tragic moments, they often disconnect from their heart, shutting down their true emotions and rejecting themselves.

During this process, I ask them to picture where their child is in the scene. They always describe the environment in great detail, too, deepening their experience of the memory. Then I ask them to invite their adult self into the scene with the inner child. We work back through the memory with their adult self fully present with their inner child during this memory. The purpose of this is for the grown-up version of the little girl or boy to listen to and validate the inner child. Going back to the memory and re-experiencing it with their nurturing and protective adult self relieves confusion, hurt, trauma, shame, and fear about the memory.

Then, I pray and invite God's presence into the memory, asking Him to shine a new light on the scene, revealing more about what happened there and where He was during this experience. He always shows up in supernatural, healing ways, encouraging and empowering the person. His presence shines His light of truth on the situation, enabling them to experience how He created them, how He loves them, and how He wants to redeem their pain.

CONNECT TO YOUR HEART

Meeting and embracing our inner child reconnects us with our own heart. This necessary first step opens the way for us to connect to God's heart, the second step of the healing process. Connecting to God's heart allows Him into the wounded spaces and broken pieces. There, He can expose the lies we have believed about ourselves, about Him, and about the painful experiences that hold us in bondage.

This is a crucial part of the process of healing. Taking our heart to the one who created it is the only way we can be healed and transformed. Deep, intimate heart-to-heart connection with Him is the only place where we can feel completely whole and fully loved. He shows us powerful, life-changing things that we couldn't see before. He wants to heal our brokenness when we turn to Him for help.

As I explain the Inner Healing Prayer process in counseling sessions, I invite God into the memories–into the painful experiences. Here He always reveals the truth so we can heal and be free from the lies of the painful event. He reminds us that though we live in a world where evil has dominion, He sees us. He knows our pain. He loves us, and He never leaves our side. He wants to heal our brokenness when we turn to Him for help.

When we were younger, we didn't understand that evil ruled over the world. We didn't know that we were opposed by Satan, our enemy, who battled every day for control over our hearts and minds. Often, our parents didn't realize it either. They may not have known how to protect us from it, thereby allowing evil to steal our innocence. God is not the author of our pain and suffering. He didn't create it, and He never intended it for us. Most importantly, He isn't leaving us there in it. He wants to connect with us.

He can only do that for us when we choose to connect with Him heart to heart, spirit to Spirit. Yet, in our pain, we often disconnect from our hearts in self-protection, not realizing that in doing so, we disconnect from the heart of God, too.

The Inner Healing Prayer process reconnects us to our heart and to the heart of God. This process also exposes the things that hinder our connection with God and the Holy Spirit. It helps us uncover the lies that keep us stuck in bondage and oppression and reveals God's supernatural truth that changes our reality. The Holy Spirit guides the experience, brings revelation, and facilitates powerful healing and transformation.

I'm convinced that the most important work God wants to do in us is the transformational breakthrough healing of our pain and restoring our hearts. It's our woundedness that keeps us stuck in bondage and struggle, and "God is mighty in pulling down strongholds," (2 Cor. 10:4 *NIV*) to "bind up the brokenhearted, to proclaim freedom for the captives, and release the prisoners from darkness." (Isaiah 61:1 *NIV*)

It breaks my heart to see so many Christians living in defeat, despair, depression, and discouragement. They believe in and know God, but they are not free. They settle for knowing about Him instead of being healed and transformed by Him. They settle for salvation without seeing His promises in their lives.

That was me for many years, too. I knew about God, but I didn't really know Him. I knew a system of religion, and I knew the rules of the religion, but I had never personally experienced God's Presence or felt His love. I didn't realize that I couldn't let God into the parts of my heart I wasn't willing to open and connect with. When I began to embrace myself fully and reconnect with all of my heart, pushing deeper into the healing process, I began to have intimate, personal encounters with God that I never knew existed. I began to feel His Presence and hear His voice, and it's in the personal encounters with God where powerful transformation happens inside of us and in our lives.

By reconnecting to my own heart and connecting to the heart of God, I have encountered His goodness, His healing power, and an experience of transformation that has begun to unravel every lie I have believed about myself and about God. I have discovered that experiencing God in a personal, intimate way brings breakthrough to every bondage, every trauma, every lie, and every assault on our life by the evil one.

As 2 Corinthians 3:17-18 (*NIV*) says, "Now the Lord is the Spirit, and where the Spirit of the Lord is, there is freedom. And we all, who with unveiled faces all reflect the Lord's glory, are being transformed into his likeness with ever-increasing glory, which comes from the Lord, who is the Spirit."

It is the presence of God's Spirit in us that liberates our body, soul, spirit. All of our bondage is broken when we encounter Him and come to know the truth of who we are, whose we are, and who He really is. Further, as we connect with Him, Spirit to spirit, we are transformed into His image with ever-increasing glory. We become like Him. We begin to see with His eyes, love with His heart, and live by His wisdom. We begin awakening to the truth of who He created us to be and the life He has for us. When we know His supernatural power that works in and through us, then we can step into a life of abundance, fulfillment, joy, peace, and love. We can then grow in our belief that nothing is impossible for God. (Luke 1:37)

DETHRONE THE COUNTERFEIT WARRIOR

There is a third step to our journey of inner healing. We must dethrone our Counterfeit Warrior so we are no longer tormented and dominated by the harsh, critical voice that incites shame, fear, and doubt in us constantly.

We have been listening to the voice of our inner critic for so long. That harsh, critical voice has become so familiar and comfortable that we come to think of it as our own. We even believe that it protects us from feeling more pain or disappointment and that it motivates us to work harder and to be better.

Now that we see and understand that our Counterfeit Warrior is not our protector, our motivator, or our friend, then we must remove him or her from the throne in our minds that we have allowed them to inhabit for so long. It is really a simple solution to a very big problem in our lives, but simple doesn't mean it's easy. We have to decide that we are tired of being lied to, threatened, and bullied, and we choose to stand up to that voice.

One of the most freeing things I have ever done was to remove my own Counterfeit Warrior, "Strong Connie," from her throne. I was sick of living with the evil tormentor in my head who ripped me apart, who reminded me of all of the times I had screwed up, and who incited fear in me that there was never going to be enough because I'm not enough. Incessantly, she whispered to me that I would always have to work harder than others and strive to be better to get what I could for myself. She said that no matter what I did, the life and love I wanted would never happen because something was wrong with me, and I would never get it right. Believing those lies and threats kept me living in prison for far too long. I had a love-hate relationship with her for many years. In a Healing Prayer Session, when the Holy Spirit revealed to me how badly she was abusing me and robbing me of life, I decided I wanted her gone.

Again, the solution was simple but getting rid of her was not easy. The voice I knew so well was loud and overbearing. She had become such an intimate part of me. I didn't realize that in trying to merely survive, I had invited her into my will to reign over my mind and my life. As a result, her voice often overpowered the voice of God in my mind. Inviting her into my will had inhibited me from discerning the voice and movement of the Holy Spirit (the two are opposing). She had armored my heart, blocking me from hearing and feeling God's love and wisdom. She hindered me from receiving or trusting love from others, too, especially an emotionally available man. She had kept me safe, but alone and isolated.

Our Counterfeit Warrior is our intimate self-destructor, and dethroning them is like killing a part of ourselves that taught us how to survive. It is not easy, but I know this for sure: the habits we create to survive will no longer serve us when it's time to thrive. When I reached the point where I desperately wanted to escape survival mode, I was willing to do whatever it took to find the abundant life that God intended for me. It was time for Strong Connie to be dethroned once and for all.

My therapist helped me understand that she wasn't just going away. She would always be there, but she could no longer reign in my life. She had been there to protect me in a crucial time when I couldn't defend myself, so I didn't have to hate her. I couldn't and didn't really want to get rid of her completely because she was a part of me and part of my story. I could thank her for doing the best she could with what she had at the time and then let her know that I didn't need her to be in charge anymore. It was time for her to retire–to sit down and rest. She was no longer allowed to have a say. During a counseling session, I "uninvited" her from my will and invited the Holy Spirit to rule in my mind, heart, and life.

As I spent time quieting myself and connecting to my heart and to God's heart, I became familiar with another voice inside of me that speaks life, is encouraging, nurturing, wise, and loving. It comes from my heart, from His Spirit in me. I realized that I can start listening to and honoring that voice instead of the voice of my harsh inner critic.

I began listening to that voice that aligned with God's truth of who I really am and His promises for me. Practicing being in His presence, hearing the new voice that I wasn't used to, took time and discipline because the harsh, critical one had been so loud and demeaning. I had to be still, quiet my mind, connect with my heart–tuning my instrument every day to resonate with His voice.

I would often picture myself at the feet of Jesus, sitting beside Him, or sometimes even in His lap. I asked Him a lot of questions, and I wrote down what I heard Him answer. In moments of confusion, I would ask myself, what would Jesus say? How would He love me in this? What would be His voice of truth?

Sometimes, I would even ask, "If I could hear the voice of my heart right now, what would it say?" And I would sit and wait until I heard it, or I would journal until I could hear it. The voice of truth and love is always there, waiting to be heard and acknowledged. We just have to open our hearts and desire to hear it more than the other voice that torments us. When we're ready, we must be diligent about silencing the other noise that drowns it out.

Hear this and take it to heart! God wants to be found by us. He wants to reveal His mysteries to us. He is speaking, and we will hear Him when we want to listen to what He has to say. Further, our hearts are always letting us know what we need–the truth is available to us at all times. It's a matter of whether we will get quiet and listen rather than staying in the habit of living in distraction, stress, and overwhelm.

At some point, though, truth no longer whispers to us in the quiet moments when we are still enough to hear. Sometimes, we move so far away from truth and become so disconnected from our hearts that the whisper becomes a roar. When I reached that point, my heart was dying inside and crying out to me. My body was breaking down and screaming at me. I couldn't ignore it anymore. It had to change.

I dedicated myself to reconnecting with my heart daily until it got easier and more comfortable. I practiced tuning in to God's voice until it became more prominent and familiar. The tone was hopeful, peaceful, and life-giving. It was calm, loving, wise, encouraging, and always aligned with Biblical truth. In a moment of struggle or doubt, it may be a hard truth, but even still, it's always loving, empowering, and freedom giving.

When we commit to the daily practice of tuning our hearts and minds into the voice of love and truth, our minds powerfully transform over time. We develop a sensitivity to the Spirit, and we gain a new perspective. This empowers us to step into a new way of being and living.

COME HOME

Embracing these steps to healing sets us on a course to wholeness. One more change will put us on the road to freedom.

Throughout my life journey, I constantly battled myself, and I resisted God's love and the story He was writing for me. The harder I tried to be who I was supposed to be and make life work for me, the greater the struggle became. This was my reality until I realized that I needed to release the image of who I thought I was and the picture of how my life should be. It was finally time to take it all and lay it down at God's feet in total surrender.

Rather than being the author of the story and the star of the show, performing all day long, we must give God the pen, allow Him to write the greater story, and take the lead. How freeing and fulfilling it is to get to know Him, to trust His plan and purpose for our lives, and rest in His goodness and favor.

At the end of the story he was writing for himself, the prodigal son came home. He learned that his answers weren't out in the world. They were inside of him, at his center, where wisdom and passion reside.

We have to come home, too, and bring all of our scattered pieces back with us. Then we can embrace and enjoy the redemption story

God is writing in our lives and watch how He propels us to more than we can imagine. The world needs our hearts. People need us to walk in our purpose, to meet a destiny that only we can fulfill, one that is beyond our wildest dreams.

REFLECTION

"He heals the brokenhearted and binds up their wounds."

—Psalm 147:3 *(NIV)*

Are you more of a critical or a nurturing parent to your inner child? How does that affect him or her? How does he/she feel as a result?

How have you disconnected from your own heart and from God's heart in self-protection? What parts of your heart have you disconnected from and why?

What parts of your heart have you shut God out of and why? What wounded spaces and broken pieces of your heart do you need to invite Him into so He can shine His light of truth there?

What painful experiences and negative messages do you need Him to illuminate with His truth?

What negative messages, lies, or criticisms does your counterfeit warrior reinforce to you?

How are you still trying to write your own story? How are you attempting to be the star of the show in your life? How are you still looking for happiness and peace in a broken world? What is the result?

APPLICATION

*"The Spirit of the Sovereign Lord is on me, because the Lord
has anointed me to proclaim good news to the poor. He has
sent me to bind up the brokenhearted, to proclaim freedom for
the captives, and release from darkness for the prisoners,
to proclaim the year of the Lord's favor and the day of
vengeance of our God, to comfort all who mourn, and provide
for those who grieve in Zion – to bestow on them a crown of
beauty instead of ashes, the oil of joy instead of mourning, and
a garment of praise instead of a spirit of despair.
They will be called oaks of righteousness, a planting of
the Lord for the display of his splendor."*

—Isaiah 61:1-3 *(NIV)*

It's time for you to gather your scattered pieces and come home. Go
back for the parts of yourself you buried underground, rejected, criticized, and shamed. Make peace with those parts.

Acknowledge, accept, and embrace your inner child. He or she has
been abandoned, rejected, and abused for long enough. Tell your
inner child that it wasn't his/her fault and the messages they received
are not true.

Right now, in Jesus' name, choose to come out of agreement with the lies you have believed about you, God, and life. Simply say, "In Jesus' name, I choose to come out of agreement with the lie that _____. I choose to come into agreement with the truth that _____.

Read the truth out loud daily until it begins to become your reality.

Also, if you have subconsciously or consciously invited your counterfeit warrior into your will to reign over your mind and your life, are you now ready to renounce him or her and invite the Holy Spirit into your will? Simply say, "I uninvite [the name of your counterfeit warrior] from my will. He or she has no authority over my mind, will, or emotions. I invite the Holy Spirit into my will to reign over my mind, will, and emotions and to rule over my heart."

Forgive yourself for not knowing what you didn't know when you were younger. Commit to learning how to treat yourself with grace and compassion. Love the special and unique creation that you are. Commit to engaging in the heart healing work that you need to do to be whole and free.

As you make peace with you, learn to love all of you. Receive healing for your heart wounds, reconnect with your heart and with God's heart. Spend time in His presence. Ask Him how He sees you. Ponder His thoughts about you. Ask Him to speak to you about who you are and what He made special about you.

Ask Him what pain and hurt He wants to heal and redeem. Now invite Him into those places in your heart and allow Him to do His supernatural heart surgery.

CHAPTER TWELVE

Warrior Awakening

*"This resurrection life you received from God is not a timid,
grave-tending life. It's adventurously expectant, greeting God
with a childlike, 'What's next, Papa?' God's Spirit touches
our spirits and confirms who we really are. We know who He
is, and we know who we are: Father and children, and
we know we are going to get what's coming to us –
an unbelievable inheritance!"*

—Romans 8:15-16 *(The Message)*

A JOYFUL HOMECOMING welcomed the prodigal son back
into his family. Wearing new clothes and his father's ring signified his
restoration, but he had to figure out his purpose. He had to make some
changes to get his life back, to live powerfully in who he was created to be.

Like the prodigal son, I was ready for a new life, but I knew I
needed to make some changes, too. There was a lot that I needed to take
responsibility for in my life and in my business. The deep spiritual and
inner healing work I had done prepared me for what was next. Now, I

was prepared to take an honest look at my challenges and to develop an action plan to move closer to the life I knew God intended for me.

Working with Kami, my life coach, helped me see my blind spots. She lives in Colorado, so we held coaching calls for an hour every two weeks. In our first session, I shared honestly and vulnerably–and desperately–my frustration with the huge gap I felt in my life and my business. Years of continually doing what I felt like I had to do, wishing things were different, left me exhausted. I told her about my vision for the life I wanted to be living, the work I preferred to do, and the impact I envisioned making on the hearts and lives of the people I worked with.

Between sessions, she gave me assignments to complete that enhanced what we had discussed during our calls.

CHANGING MY LIFE

I explained to Kami that I knew I was gifted as a therapist to help people break free from thought and behavior patterns that imprison and hinder them from living in their authentic selves and the destiny God intended for them. I attracted bright, capable, successful clients that I enjoyed working with. They came to see me for relational counseling or to address a personal issue or stressor. Many sought help for addictive or compulsive behaviors that kept them stuck or for guidance in transforming some aspects of their lives or work.

We would begin working on the personal and relational issues and then delve into their career and business struggles. The personal struggles always bled over into their professional lives, and vice-versa. I've never understood how the two can be separated and compartmentalized. Helping people create positive change in all areas of their lives is what I enjoy doing most.

I loved seeing my clients make powerful transformations. There was no doubt that I was called to continue doing that work, but it was exhausting and frustrating to see client after client one-on-one in the numbers that I needed to meet my monthly expenses. There was nothing left over for retirement, saving, travel, or living much at all after the bills were paid.

Further, I found that many of my clients experienced similar struggles. I saw many recurring themes. I longed to have the time and energy to assimilate the knowledge and wisdom I had gathered over ten years of counseling so that I could help more than one person at a time.

The counseling work I had been doing for years already incorporated a lot of coaching into it, as I helped people move forward in their lives, relationships, and businesses. I wanted to share this breakthrough knowledge with people in larger arenas, teaching and speaking in workshops and seminars, creating and teaching coaching groups, and even writing the books that were burning inside of me. To do that, I needed to engage in the business community, but I had no time or energy left for that after counseling clients one-on-one all day.

Finally, I wanted to be living a life I loved, a life that was true to who I was and what was most important to my heart. I longed to be in community with like-minded and like-hearted people. I wanted to work out and play tennis, have time to take care of myself, to deepen my relationships, enjoy my friends, date, and travel. Desperate for change, I thought about how to close those gaps in my life all day, every day. Figuring out how to make it all happen felt overwhelming, scary, and far out of reach. The dreams I wholeheartedly believed God put in my heart were dying inside of me more and more every day.

Fortunately for me, Kami had gone through a similar experience several years earlier, and she had successfully transitioned into doing what she loved and living the life she desired. I hoped that she knew how to help me do that in my own life and work, and I dedicated myself fully to a year-long transformation process.

Kami's coaching helps people reconnect with who they are–their natural strengths, gifts, values, passions, and life purpose–so they can center and create their life and work out of their true essence. She also coaches women to raise their voice, visibility, and business so they can make the impact they want to make in the world. Like I do, she believes that when you are living true to your authentic self and connected to your heart, you are most effective, successful, and fulfilled. You are your best and happiest you. Then your career and business are an expression of your true essence and your passion and purpose.

In our first few sessions, we completed several coaching exercises that required me to take a deep dive into my heart and my truth. Kami helped me identify my strengths, gifts, values, and priorities. The discovery process was soul-searching and gut-wrenching, but it was life-giving, too. I realized that I had thrown myself into work to avoid the emptiness and loneliness inside. My addiction to achievement and desperate need for approval numbed my heart. I stayed busy fixing everybody else's lives, never acknowledging the deep pain I felt inside.

As I began to quiet my spirit and listen to what my heart was saying, I experienced a powerful awakening. For as many years as I could remember, I strived to be the person I thought I should be, but I lived a life that wasn't really mine. Struggling to follow strategies and formulas that seemed to work for others was just creating more work, exhaustion, and frustration for me. Most importantly, I disregarded my internal superpowers–my inner wisdom, discernment, and intuition–and was not living in my natural rhythm.

I realigned with the passions that had been steadily present throughout my life–relationships and connections, animals, nature, art, movement, and creative expression, all woven together with a large thread of spirituality.

DISCOVERING MY PURPOSE

Reconnecting to my passions was a vital part of the process of discovering my life purpose. Following several months of deep reflection, clarity about who I am and what I'm created for emerged from the center of my heart for the first time in my life. One of Kami's coaching exercises on discovering my purpose prompted me to write this truth statement. Every word is sacred because I know God breathed this into me. Each one is congruent with who I am, and I often read it as a reminder of truth.

I am a passionate, brave, fierce, loving, adventurous, free-spirited Empath who lives in alignment with my heart and spirit. I am nourished by the beauty of nature and animals. I thrive in connecting with people's hearts and their unique stories. My life's mission is to know God intimately and to live out the beautiful story that He is writing in my life. I am a beloved daughter of God, grounded in His truth and abundant love. As a Warrior Princess, I live victoriously over the darkness that battles for my heart. I inspire, empower, and equip others to win the battle for their hearts so they can live and lead bravely, freely, and authentically in their destiny!

During our next coaching call, I read my truth statement aloud to Kami. I could actually hear her smiling over the phone. When I finished reading, she said, "You're a Heart Warrior! You're a warrior for people's hearts!"

Simultaneous chills and a fire burning in my belly accompanied this truth as it resonated deeply in my soul. Everything began to make sense. The things I was passionate about and the purpose God had gifted me were meshing together. I could see how all of the pieces of my story, even the most painful, disappointing ones, had shaped me into the person God created me to be and the destiny He created me to fulfill.

All these years, I had believed that my heart was my greatest weakness, my biggest problem, and I wished so many days I could shut it off and just not care so much. I would pray for God to take away what I felt was an evil curse–feeling the pain and brokenness of others and of the world as well as feeling my own. This new revelation helped me see that what I had believed to be a curse was actually my greatest gift.

God had given me the gift of the heart. Gratitude and humility overwhelmed me! I couldn't imagine a more beautiful blessing or a better gift, even though living it out means engaging in a daily battle with darkness.

I no longer felt punished by God or odds with myself about who I was or wasn't. The long-term, strategic deception, and opposition from the enemy was fully exposed. As long as I believed that what God had put in me was less than what He gave to others, I felt cheated, neglected, and insignificant. As long as I was ensnared in the trap of that lie, I would remain in slavery, wandering in the wilderness, never reaching my destiny.

Understanding the truth freed me from that prison and launched me wholeheartedly into my purpose. I felt a renewed passion for helping people heal their hearts and transform their lives. It was now clear how crucial it was for me to war not only for my heart but for the hearts and the lives of so many others. God confirmed to me that He was sending many more to me to set free.

Discovering that I am a Heart Warrior put some other pieces together for me, too. I'd always loved and collected hearts, arrows, arrowheads, and angels. I was drawn to them naturally because they connected to my deepest passions and my life purpose. It's no coincidence. My heart knew it all along. I cherish the clients God anoints and appoints me to work with. He confirms to me why He personally assigned each one to me and there is no greater honor and privilege.

The discovery of my true essence and purpose was extra special to me because now that I know how much God values my heart, that means I can value it, too. Because my heart is the most valuable part of me, I can trust it. As long as my heart is fully submitted and connected to my Creator God, it is my very own superpower–my intuition is a sixth sense that I can trust. This is where the Spirit of God resides, revealing His wisdom and mysteries, imparting supernatural courage so that through me, His truth and love can heal and transform people's hearts and lives.

With this awakening, I also received clarity and understanding about why, a few years earlier, when I read these verses I felt moved to my core by their power:

"The Spirit of the Lord God is upon me, because the Lord has anointed me to bring good news to the afflicted; He has sent me to bind up the brokenhearted, to proclaim liberty to captives and freedom to prisoners; To proclaim the favorable year of the Lord and the day of vengeance of our God." —Isaiah 61:1-2 *(NIV)*

Doesn't that sound like a true Heart Warrior to you? It does to me! Since then, God has revealed more to me about my purpose. In a powerful encounter, He replaced the lies I believed about who I was with my true identity as His "daughter." In connection and communion with Him, I found my enoughness, my significance. He gave me the freedom to be who He had created me to be.

He whispered into my spirit: "You are my Warrior and my

Wildflower. Natural and untamed. Wild and free. I don't need you to be anyone else or do it all right. I created you in my image, and I need you to be exactly who you are. I love you for the unique way I created you."

God showed me that there is nothing wrong with me. I am not less of a person. I'm not on the outside. I'm not left out of His favor. I don't have to do it all right. He is pleased with me and loves me dearly. He showed me the seat beside Him that was saved for me.

I pictured myself handing over the big mess I thought I had made of my life. In place of these ashes of inadequacy, He planted a beautiful garden of wildflowers.

He said:

"Con, you are the beauty of my heart. You see my beauty all around, and you reflect it to others."

In that moment, gratitude welled up inside me as He gave me a clear vision of my life purpose. As a Heart Warrior, I help people live victoriously over darkness. I inspire, empower, and equip people to live and lead bravely, freely, and authentically. I see and reflect the beauty of God's heart so that others can know and experience Him and live in their true identity and fulfill their destiny.

LIVING FULLY ALIVE

Aligning with my passion and discovering my purpose also clarified what was most important to me, how I wanted to spend my time and energy, and the impact I wanted to make in the world. I intentionally shifted my activities to engage my passions, a direction that required some brave and bold decisions.

The real me re-emerged as I came back to life. Little by little, I noticed and reconnected with the things that made me happy. I incorporated them into my life–things like connecting with people and with the beauty and wonder of nature and animals. I also realized how important movement, creative expression, holistic health, and nutrition were to me during this time. I had always been happiest, healthiest, and most connected to my body and spirit when I practiced healthy self-care.

I discovered that I am an Empath, so I began to recognize the importance of monitoring and balancing the flow of energy into and out of my body. I started seeing a functional medicine doctor to heal my adrenal and thyroid glands and balance my hormones. They were all negatively affected by the mental, emotional, and chemical stress I had been under for years.

Further, I knew the Daytrana had taken a toll on my body, so I began weaning myself off of it. It was a long, hard three-year battle, riddled with chronic pain, inflammation, exhaustion, and even more complex chemical imbalances. Old eating disorder thoughts and behaviors surfaced. As tough as it was, I stayed committed to my truth and to the pursuit of wellness. In the end, the victory was well worth the fight. I realized quickly that it had caused me to live in a constant state of fight or flight for all those years I was on it. Finally, I was allowed to slow down, heal, rest, and learn to nurture and nourish my body, mind, and spirit. My dependence on and trust in God was strengthened because I could no longer live and work at the frenetic pace I always had.

I began fueling my body with healthier, whole foods, working with a nutrition coach for support and accountability. I also incorporated running, deep stretching, and breathing into my day, started CrossFit, and began playing tennis again.

I attended a couple of retreats at Kami's ranch in Colorado, where she does equine coaching. I was drawn to the majesty and magic of horses, so I attended several other retreats in Arizona with a group of friends who shared my passion. I enjoyed the personal growth and

inner awakenings that the horses offered so much that I even participated in an equine coaching training for a week in California. These
were all memorable and life-shifting experiences.

I re-engaged with people, old friends and new ones that God
brought to me. I participated in a women's Bible study, joined a
running group, volunteered at my church, and joined several other
business organizations with like-minded and like-hearted leaders in
our community. I smiled and laughed more. Friends said I sparkled.
Every day, I soaked up with gratitude the beauty of creation all around
me. The best way to describe it is that I was, finally, fully alive!

I grew more in this period of awakening and uncaging than in my
first forty years of life. Though the journey was long and hard and often
scary and painful, the freedom I've experienced has been well worth
every struggle. I've blown through barriers I never thought possible,
and my breakthroughs expanded my capacity, enhanced my relationships, and catapulted my career and business.

My inner Warrior has awakened, and she is rising up to be the
powerful Warrior Princess that God destined me to be. The wisdom
I've gained and the tools I've learned throughout my journey are so
transformational that I'm compelled to share it with others.

As a result of my powerful life transformation, a shift in my work
occurred, too. Kami helped me clarify my vision for my business. Then
we created and implemented a dream-to-action plan. My dream was
to transition to a unique and powerful combination of counseling
and coaching for people who want to awaken to their true essence
and discover their God-given purpose. I help them uncage from the
mindsets and patterns that hinder them from living bravely, freely, and
authentically in the life God created for them.

My vision also included coaching entrepreneurs, executives, and
leaders who yearn to live and lead with courage and authenticity but

who are trapped in performance, achievement, fear, self-doubt, scarcity, and overwhelm. Many lack clarity about their "why." They settle for struggling, striving, and surviving in their work and business, but they crave freedom, fulfillment, and prosperity and don't know how to unlock it. Many dream of making a greater impact and influence, but they feel stuck in a much smaller and harder existence. The reason I love this work is obvious–this is my story, too! I know I can help them get the breakthrough they need so they can soar at new levels of success and satisfaction in life, work, and business!

In addition to the one-on-one counseling and coaching work with my clients, my dream included hosting retreats, facilitating coaching groups and seminars, and spiritual discipleship/coaching for leaders, all of which have happened. I even co-facilitated an equine coaching retreat with Kami in Colorado. That was a special trip for so many reasons.

I want to speak, teach, and coach on a larger scale on various platforms. I have several books in me just waiting to be birthed, and I am planning to launch my online coaching courses, podcast, and coaching mastermind for entrepreneurs this year. Now, with more margin with my time and energy, I can make these dreams my reality, too.

While writing this first one, I created the Warrior Arise! Tribe community group on Facebook, where I share daily inspiration, empowerment, and encouragement with men and women who want to thrive in a life of freedom and fullness. On Warrior Wednesdays, I live-stream to teach people how to live The Warrior Way. My weekly Heart Spark vlogs also empower and inspire people. As a motivational speaker, I impart hope to my audiences through sharing my journey of struggle and victory along with wisdom from almost twenty years of experience as a therapist and coach.

My passion for living out my purpose burns brighter than ever, and I've only begun. The dreams and vision God put in my heart and mind are so much bigger than anything I could ever begin to create or develop on my own. I can't wait to see how He brings them to fruition.

God is the Great Warrior, and we are His beloved children, made in His likeness. Inside each of us is a Warrior waiting to awaken and arise. My fellow Warriors, now is the time!

REFLECTION

*"We have become His poetry, a re-created people that will
fulfill the destiny He has given each of us, for we are joined to
Jesus, the Anointed One. Even before we were born,
God planned in advance our destiny and the good
works we would do to fulfill it!"*

—Ephesians 2:10 (*TPT*)

What is your dream for the life you want to be living and the work you want to be doing? What impact do you want to make in the world? Do you feel, like I did, as if your dreams are dying inside of you?

What do you need to take responsibility for changing in your life that will move you closer to the more God has for you? In your work? In your business?

What do you long to have more time and energy for?

Why are you choosing to live the life that you are? Do you feel disconnected from your heart, intuition, discernment?

What self-sabotaging behaviors are keeping you stuck? What is the true longing that you are masking?

If it's true that change comes with great inspiration or great pain and desperation, then are you really ready for change? What are you willing to do for it?

Do you know your natural strengths, gifts, values, and priorities? Are you connected to and aligned with your passions? Do you know your life purpose? If the answer is no, but you'd like to explore this, reach out to me from www.warriorarise.com.

APPLICATION

*"So we are convinced that every detail of our lives is
continually woven together to fit into God's perfect plan of
bringing good into our lives, for we are His lovers who have
been called to fulfill His designed purpose."*

—Romans 8:28 (TPT)

You are a beloved child of God. You are gifted with unique passions
and a specific purpose – a destiny to fulfill that no one else can. You
have special gifts, a seed God put inside of you to grow and share with
the world that is all your own. You are created with a special power and
capability that, unleashed, will bring forth your calling. You have the
ability within you to bring forth your supernatural gift–your unique
piece of God's heart that only you have.

Imagine your power as your light within. Allow your light to rekindle
and begin to burn brightly inside.

Remember a time in your life you experienced your light shining
brightly. How differently would you live if your light was shining
bright, and you allowed your inner fire to be rekindled?

What lights your fire?

What do you burn for?

Your light is God's greatness in you—His supernatural power and purpose He put there. If you were to tap into it and let it burn, what passions would rise up in you?

What squelches your passion and dims your light?

You are a powerful, divine being. You are most powerful when you live in your true essence and live out your passion and purpose. Within you, there is a powerful Warrior waiting to awaken. Will you answer the call?

Are you ready to live, work, and lead with passion, purpose, and meaning? Join our growing tribe of like-minded, kindred souls who are determined to live a life of freedom and fullness. Search for Warrior Arise! Tribe on Facebook.

PART THREE

Warrior Arise!

CHAPTER THIRTEEN

Winning the War in Your Mind

"Stop imitating the ideals and opinions of the culture around you, but be inwardly transformed by the Holy Spirit through a total reformation of how you think. This will empower you to discern God's will as you live a beautiful life, satisfying and perfect in His eyes."

—Romans 12:2 *(THE MIRROR)*

AS I ENVISIONED THE GREATNESS inside of me rising up and waiting to be unleashed, I considered what it would look and feel like to show up as my best self in my best life. I connected deeply with those thoughts, feelings, and visualizations, transcribing every detail of every aspect of my life. An exhaustive inventory of all of the dreams in my heart poured onto paper, and as it did, my hope and excitement surged.

But the thrill was short-lived. No more than an hour later, reviewing what I had written, negative thoughts overwhelmed me. Doubt, fear, and shame bombarded my mind with loud, intrusive accusations.

"That'll never happen for you." "You want too much." "That's self-ish." "Maybe that's not what God wants for you." "You shouldn't be such a dreamer. That's not realistic." "How's that ever going to happen when you're already 40 years old, and you're single, AND you've made all those bad decisions." "You're greedy. You just need to be content with what you have and not always want more." "You aren't deserving." On and on these negative thoughts rolled, stealing a little more hope from me every moment I allowed them to continue.

Thank God I shared the list with Kami in one of our coaching sessions, so she could speak truth and life back into my dreams. Otherwise, they would have dead-ended right there on my paper. During that session and over the next several months, I developed a firsthand understanding of an important truth.

When we reconnect to our heart, when we ignite our passion and feel even a sliver of hope about the dreams God put in us, our enemy retaliates with arrows of doubt, fear, and shame. Often we fall back to the small existence we've always known, deflected again from the life we were meant to live. The more passionate I became about unleashing the free and full life that God created me for, the harder the enemy fought to hold me in slavery to struggle and survival-mode.

Some of the hardest battles we fight are in our minds. Doubt, fear, and shame blind us to freedom and to the more God has for us. Negative, limiting thoughts keep us stuck, miserable, and frustrated. They cycle over and over like dirty laundry in a washing machine. To step out of our misery, we must replace those old messages with new scripts. The ones we've always used will get us exactly where we've always been and nowhere else. I was learning how important reprogramming my negative mindsets was in coaching sessions with Kami. I had no idea that I was about to close the gap between defeat and victory on the battlefield of my mind.

One evening, as I came home from work, I walked in the door to find Bridgett and Carol sitting in the living room talking. It was customary for us to visit in the evenings and discuss our day, what events took place, and especially what God had revealed to each of us during the day on our journey to the breakthrough we were fervently seeking in our lives.

That evening, Bridgett and Carol told me about a little booklet they had discovered by Charles Capps, called *God's Creative Power*. A psychiatrist friend had given the booklet to me for Christmas, but I hadn't gotten around to reading it. Bridgett often would look through my stack of books and find ones she wanted to read that I wasn't currently reading. I had told her she could have that one since I didn't have time to read it. At the time, I was focused on other readings and studying. Little did I know that this tiny booklet was the next step to the breakthrough that God wanted to show me. I would have missed it if Bridgett had not been so hungry and faithful to check it out.

She began to share with me what it was about. The truths she shared from this booklet were eye-opening. I read it that evening, and it all made so much sense.

WORDS OF FAITH

Mr. Capps shared that because we are both physical and spiritual beings, we have within us the same creative power that God used to create everything in the Universe. This power is released in our spoken words.

Christianity is often called the great confession, Mr. Capps points out. Unfortunately, many Christians live defeated because of the things they believe and speak, either to others or themselves. Instead of speaking the life-giving truths aligned with the word of God, we give voice to the accusations of the enemy. It's no wonder we live in bondage.

Understanding that truth clarifies the meaning of Proverbs 6:2 *(NIV)*, "You have been trapped by what you said, ensnared by the words of your mouth."

It's important for us to understand that because we have God's Spirit in us, our words have authority. Mr. Capps reminds us that God releases His faith in His spoken word. He says what He will do before He does it. Every time.

Just as God released faith in words when He created all of the universe, Jesus imitated His Father when he performed miracles like calming the wind with a word, raising Lazarus from the dead, cursing the fig tree, and more. Jesus says in Matthew 17:20: "Truly I tell you, if you have faith as small as a mustard seed, you can say to this mountain, 'Move from here to there,' and it will move. Nothing will be impossible for you." *(NIV)*

In John 14:12, Jesus said, "Very truly I tell you, whoever believes in me will do the works I have been doing, and they will do even greater things than these…" *(NIV)*

These principles of faith are based on spiritual laws. We set faith in motion by the words of our mouth.

Romans 10:17 says, "So then faith comes by hearing and hearing by the Word of God." *(NKJV)* Faith, then, comes more quickly when you hear yourself quoting, speaking, and saying the things God said.

When Mr. Capps emphasized that our words are vessels that carry faith or fear which produce more of their same kind, this new truth fired me up! I wasn't about to put the book down now. This was such an answer to prayer–and it was going to be life-changing–I hoped!

I asked myself if I really want all the negative things I have been saying to come to pass. Was I believing for those things? If Jesus came to me and said that everything I said moving forward would happen exactly as I say it, would I change what I speak? Um, yes! That's an easy answer. Absolutely, I would!

In Psalms 119:89, we read, "Forever, O Lord, Your word is firmly fixed in the heavens." *(ESV)*

What God said is already established. He doesn't alter what He says! He doesn't break His covenants! So, it's up to me to align my words with His truth to establish what He says on earth.

Mr. Capps pointed out that Jesus used God's word by praying the answer–what God said–rather than the problem. He spoke what God said, verbalizing the desired results rather than present circumstances. "It is written," Jesus said, over and over again to Pharisees, Satan, and his accusers. This final realization sealed the deal for me!

Man, alive, was I beside myself in excitement! I couldn't believe I had never heard these truths before. But it made so much sense. I knew in my Spirit it was true and that God had led me to this revelation.

I read it over and over and then ordered a couple of other books by Charles Capps and read those, too. As I soaked it all in, I realized that when I agree with what God has said about me and what He says He's doing in my life, my faith increases greatly when my thoughts and words align with His truth. My circumstances will begin to change to line up with what He says!

I also learned that thinking and speaking doubt-filled, negative words had to stop. We reap what we sow, Capps says. So which do we want to plant? Seeds of doubt and fear or seeds of faith and victory? We need to be sure we are planting a crop we want to harvest.

Wow! I knew what I was thinking and speaking into my life had to change for my life to change, and it was time to finally take ownership of my words.

WE ARE WHAT WE SAY

A light bulb came on for me as I read and studied this material. I began to understand that God's promises for us to live in freedom and abundance are powerful, they are true, and they are waiting to manifest in our lives. We are holding them up and choosing a different reality for ourselves because we choose to partner with fear and doubt in our thinking and speaking. Instead of focusing on what we feel and what we see as our current reality, we must begin to think and speak God's truths and promises over our life. As we focus on these truths and promises and proclaim them boldly in our lives, we create a new reality that aligns with what God says. This is exactly what Jesus did.

After reading Mr. Capp's book, I realized how frequently I thought and spoke negative words. I would say things like, "I can't have what I want. It'll never happen for me." "Everybody else gets to have or be (whatever it was in the moment), and I don't." "I always have to work harder than everybody else to get half of what they have." "I'm always alone." "I can't do what they can do."

The more I rehearsed those thoughts in my mind, and the more those words came out of my mouth, the more I received exactly what I spoke. It was a self-fulfilling prophecy. What I believed and said became the reality in my life. I solidified it every day more and more as my truth, but I couldn't see it. I blamed God for not loving me, not caring about or helping me, and for punishing me. I couldn't see that I was doing it to myself by agreeing with what was not from Him. Partnering instead with the evil one was robbing and destroying the destiny God intended for me. As this truth resonated in my heart and mind, I stopped blaming God, stopped blaming myself, and felt relieved of the shame and hopelessness. I began to shift my energy and focus on renewing my mind and changing the words I spoke.

Jesus was our model for this way of living. He was intimately connected with God, and He disciplined Himself to align His thoughts and spoken word with God's truth. He overcame negativity, doubt, fear, and sin and lived as a powerful victor, not an enslaved victim.

He showed us how, and through the power of the Holy Spirit in us, we can live this way, too. We have the same authority within us that Jesus had, but we must make a choice and be willing to do the work to tap into it and unleash it. We have to shift how we function. We must receive what the Spirit is doing until our thoughts and feelings catch up to the new truth. We can then act on it in new ways and see a fresh reality manifest in our spirits, thoughts, and lives.

Instead of complaining and speaking what the devil says, we must speak what God says is true, praying in faith. Instead of operating in fear and unbelief, establishing the words of the evil one on our behalf, we must change our confessions and agree with the truth of God's word. Instead of releasing our enemy with our words, manifesting darkness and destruction, we can unleash the power of God by confessing declarations of truth daily. These truth-filled statements build up our faith over time and become our new truth.

Scientific research confirms that as we think on and speak the things that God says about us, we create new neural pathways in our brain. The more we think positive truths, the more well-worn that path in our brain becomes, empowering us to expand those thoughts and create that reality even more in our lives. Conversely, when we think about negative things, nothing changes in our circumstances. We stay on the well-worn path of wandering in the wilderness or in bondage to addictions and compulsions.

We are divine beings, powerful creators in our lives. What we speak, we create. Diligently disciplining ourselves to declare God's promises and truths cultivates a new reality. This requires a daily practice of feeding our mind truth while starving it of fear and doubt. The truth ignites in us, burning away dead and broken undergrowth, clearing a path toward our promised land. Faith takes root where fear and doubt once reigned.

Charles Capps included in his booklets numerous statements that aligned with God's word about who we really are, about what He's done for us, and about what is available to us. It's essential to speak, out loud, these scriptures as declarations every day, even several times a day, until we feel and see change. It's like exercising, transforming the body by building muscle and starving fat. I have to do the same thing with my mind and my spoken word.

The key to change is to speak what God says about us and to speak our dreams as if they are already true. The words we speak direct our emotions, our thoughts, and our path. Even though we don't see them manifested yet, making a daily practice of these declarations powerfully transforms our minds. We fuel our fire, change our beliefs from the inside out, and ignite action that changes our reality. The repetition infuses our hearts and minds with wisdom. We know where our focus should be every day and how to spend our time and energy.

Hearing ourselves declare the truth also changes our perspective. The words we speak direct our emotions, our thoughts, and our path. As we align our thoughts and spoken words with the truth of who God says we are, who He says He is, and what He says He is doing or has already done for us, then we are transformed from the inside out.

Bridgett and I committed to this daily practice for the next few months. We spent time in prayer and worship, walking around the living room every morning declaring the truth of who we are, the truth of who God is, and His promises for our lives. We read the scripturally based declarations in the booklet, and we also looked up several other verses we were choosing to believe would manifest in our lives. We personalized them for our specific circumstances. Then we declared those, too.

Many days, we didn't want to do it. Some days, I had a hard time opening my mouth to say the words out loud. That's how strong the devil's power had been over my mind and my words. Sometimes I felt like a fake, as if I was lying to say things when I don't believe them. Yet, as long as my thoughts and words stayed the same, I remained miserable.

I knew that I was in a battle and that this was the way to overcome and win. I had to. Fortunately, when I struggled with doubt or unbelief or when I had trouble speaking, Bridgett would help me through it, and vice versa. I'm grateful I had someone to walk it out with because it was tough until I began to see the breakthrough.

I spoke to my debt, declaring in Jesus' name and on the authority of His Holy Word that my debts were paid in full, canceled, or dissolved. Over the next year, I paid off $50,000 in debt and was debt-free except for my house and my car.

A few years later, when it was time to move into a new home, I began speaking to my house and declaring it to be a blessing to some-one and calling it sold in Jesus' name. Two days before it was going on the market, a man walked up to my door and asked to buy my house. An investor in the neighborhood, he paid me what I wanted for my home without the hassle of putting it on the market or paying a real estate agent's fees. Further, after a year of declarations, I moved to a beautiful piece of property and into a home that met all of my family's needs. I had dreamed of and visualized for a couple of years living on several acres of beautiful, wide open space land, on a lake surrounded by animals and the beauty of nature. That's exactly the property that found me when the timing was perfect.

I spoke new friendships and business connections into my life, which were meaningful and fulfilling. My dating life accelerated, too, as quality, Godly men crossed my path. I also declared victory over some health issues and over the next couple of years, my body was healed and restored. Fear no longer ruled me and lack no longer tormented me. I began traveling more and enjoying life.

My income increased significantly as well. The business expanded and profited, as did my impact and influence–exponentially–as I aligned my thoughts and words with God's promise of abundance and favor and opened my heart to receive the blessings He intended for me.

We have a choice. To create something different, we must believe and speak something different. Stepping into our power, authority, and true inheritance requires that we go through an inner revolution. We need to align our hearts and minds with what the Creator of the Universe says is true, not what we see in front of us.

The process takes time, and it's not magic. It's a discipline. Many declarations I am still speaking today have not yet been realized, but I believe for them every day and I know they will manifest in God's timing as my faith continues to grow.

REFLECTION

"… Put off your old self, which belongs to your former manner of life and is corrupt through deceitful desires, and to be renewed in the spirit of your minds, and to put on the new self, created after the likeness of God in true righteousness and holiness."

—Ephesians 4:22-24 *(ESV)*

How does the statement "many Christians live defeated because of the things they believe and speak, either to others or themselves" shift your perspective? What lies of the enemy have you been speaking into your life?

If Jesus came to you and said that everything you say moving forward will happen exactly as you say it, would you change what you speak? How would it change specifically?

If words are vessels that carry faith or fear, what are your words carrying? What are they creating in your life?

What are you hindering from happening in your life because you partner with fear and doubt in your thinking and speaking? What negative thoughts and words are you rehearsing that are creating a self-fulfilling prophecy?

Are you ready and willing to align your thoughts and spoken words with the truth of God's word so you can create powerful transformation in your life?

APPLICATION

*"Be renewed in your innermost mind. This will cause
you to be completely reprogrammed in the way
you think about yourself."*

—Ephesians 4:23 (THE MIRROR)

Let's get started!

What is one area in your life where you feel stuck and desperate for a breakthrough? What have you been believing and speaking about it? What does God say is His truth about it?

Look up and choose a minimum of five scriptures that address that area of your life. Write these on a sheet of paper or in your prayer journal.

Spend time in prayer asking God what He wants you to know specifically about His promise and truth for you in that area. Write what you hear on paper or in your prayer journal.

Write these as complete sentences, in first person, and make them as specific as you can to your situation. Declare what you desire as your new reality. Write them as if they are already your reality even though you can't see it yet.

Commit to declaring out loud these statements or declarations daily for ninety days. Speak them out loud several times a day. Even when you don't believe them and don't feel like it, choose to speak them anyway. Declare them with power, authority, and confidence. Continue to declare them until they build up your faith and transform your belief.

SAMPLE DECLARATIONS

Following are variations of some of the declarations I speak over my life daily. These are a foundation upon which you can build scriptural truths you speak over your own life. Make them your own!

I am like a tree planted by rivers of water. I bear fruit in my season. My leaves will not wither and whatever I do prospers. The grace of God even makes my mistakes to prosper.

I am calm and peaceful. The joy of the Lord is my strength. Circumstances don't upset me. I rise above obstacles and make them into opportunities. God fights my battles, and I live victoriously in Him.

I am chosen, loved, valued, and favored. I am custom-made and extraordinary, God's masterpiece. I am worthy of my inheritance as a co-heir with Christ.

I am free to be me and do what I love. Blessing, favor, and prosperity flow easily to me.

Money comes to me easily and effortlessly. I have more than enough to pay bills and do what aligns with my purpose and passion.

I am whole, healthy, and well. My body is a gift and a temple. All of my cells function in the perfection in which they were created to function.

I am married to a Godly husband or wife. We honor, cherish, and respect each other, loving from God's love for us. We share openly, vulnerably, and honestly and enjoy deep intimate connection and fun adventures together.

God will do exceedingly abundantly above all that I ask or think. As I honor Him, His blessings chase me down and overtake me. I am in the right place at the right time. God's favor surrounds me.

I say a big "yes" to all the possibilities for my life and business. I open to receive God's blessings and I accept help and support from others so I can be my best me and live in my destiny.

I am grateful and thankful that every circumstance in my life is happening FOR me. I am growing and expanding in each moment as I respond from an empowered, abundant mindset.

CHAPTER FOURTEEN

Mental Strongholds

"The weapons we fight with are not the weapons of the world. On the contrary, they have divine power to demolish strongholds. We demolish arguments and every pretension that sets itself up against the knowledge of God, and we take captive every thought to make it obedient to Christ."

—2 Corinthians 10:3-5 *(THE MIRROR)*

ONCE I CHOSE TO BELIEVE and speak words that carried faith, things started shifting. My mind and my reality began to line up with the truth and began to move in the direction of my words. When we persevere in this daily discipline, we will see forward movement in our lives.

When my eyes opened to the power that our minds have to create our reality, God gave me more clarity about the battlefield of our minds. I noticed several common patterns of thinking had dominated my mind for years. Many of these same mindsets, I observed, kept many of my clients stuck and playing small in their lives, relationships, finances, careers, and businesses. We embrace these patterns of thinking in our attempts to survive in life, and they work well for us as long as we want to remain where we've always been. But when we awaken to the life we were intended to live, they are no longer effective. It's not enough to merely survive. We were made to thrive.

To defend our dreams and unlock our destiny, we must get to the core of the mental strongholds our oppressor viciously defends. You can be sure that there is a lie at the root of every stronghold, and where there is a lie, you'll always find a counterfeit warrior guarding the territory. To silence the oppressive voice in my head once and for all and to help my clients win the battle of their minds I knew those strongholds had to be torn down. The battle was daily. Fortunately, the battle belongs to the Lord, and He demolishes our enemy's base camp.

To step into our inheritance, we must unleash a full-out war on these mindsets to break their grip on us. When we recognize an area in which we are struggling to change, we must battle that ineffective pattern of thinking with the power and authority of the Warrior within.

Let's take a look at the most common mental strongholds that keep us living a stuck, small existence.

DOUBT

Doubt is the first mental stronghold that binds us to the way we've always lived. Doubt lies to us about what is available to us. It tells us our dreams will never happen, that we will never have what our heart desires. The evidence from our past reinforces those lies. When we focus on disappointments and painful experiences, we swallow that lie and settle for what feels safe and secure. We choose what we currently have or a path we see that we can create for ourselves.

I doubted for many years that I could show up as my authentic self and pursue the life and work my heart dreamed of. Until I awakened to how the lies of doubt had stolen my identity and destiny, I remained in bondage to a limited existence, resolving to do the best I could. When I rallied my Warrior within, confirming who I was and whose I was, and made the decision to replace doubt with faith, things began to shift. It wasn't a quick and easy road to freedom. I'm still walking it out, but choosing new beliefs to cling to, speak out loud, and take action on everyday starves and shrinks the power of doubt in my mind.

FEAR

Fear is the mental stronghold that always accompanies doubt. We are bullied by the lies of fear when we don't understand God's perfect love for us. When we are in fear, we believe that God, others, and our environment are not loving or supportive of us.

This puts us in fight or flight mode. We fight, flight, or freeze, experiencing stress, a permeating issue in our lives. Fear grows as we see a future with no solutions. Fear hijacks our thoughts and our emotional center. It overtakes us.

Overwhelming fear bullied me unrelentingly all of my life. When I began to see it for what it really is and identify its familiar old lies, I began to confront fear with the power and authority of the truth of God's word, which is mighty in pulling down the stronghold of fear. (2 Corinthians 10:4)

I weakened the voice of fear by speaking life and truth into my circumstances until my belief, courage, and new reality lined up with what is true. I also began to take courageous action in my life, actions that were diametrically opposed to the things I feared. I took time off that didn't seem to be there. I transformed my business model, even though it was scary. I shifted my priorities to take care of me even though I felt like I wouldn't be able to pay my bills if I did. I shared myself in more profound, meaningful ways with others, even though I was afraid of being hurt and rejected.

Amazingly, so many of the things that I was so terrified of happening never did. In fact, the opposite transpired. I became happier, healthier, more successful, and more fulfilled.

When we activate our Warrior within, we take courageous action to confront and conquer the bully of fear. We step boldly and bravely into the life we were made for and in the direction of our dreams.

SHAME

Shame is the third mental stronghold that serves as a barrier to true happiness and fulfillment. Shame attacks our identity by telling us, "You aren't worthy. You don't deserve it." "You should have." "You shouldn't have." "You're a failure." "You're too much." "You're not enough."

When we feel shame, we withdraw, hide, silence our voice, disconnect, and self-protect. We also resort to people-pleasing, approval-seeking, perfectionism, and performing. When we are in shame, we aren't showing up fully in our authentic selves, and we aren't living our truth.

When we think about stepping out courageously into the life or work that brings us alive, shame bathes us in insecurity. Shame wants us to achieve, please, and perform.

Shame keeps us trying to do enough to be enough. It is our personal brand of "Not Enough," which sends us careening into the comparison trap, where we research other people's lives trying to figure out how to be who they are, to get what they have, or do what they do. We compare ourselves to someone else's highlight reel. We assume that what they have is perfect and that we are inadequate and can't get it right. Comparison stole peace and joy from me for many years. It perpetuated a constant battle with myself and with God, and ongoing struggle and frustration in my life for way too long.

The extent that shame negatively affects each of us is different, but we all have it. We must decide to stop allowing shame to steal all the goodness God has for us.

We can break the mental stronghold of shame when we recognize the lies it feeds us. Then, we must do our inner work to heal the lies of shame and replace them daily with the truth of our significance.

SCARCITY

The fourth mental stronghold that prevents us from living the life of freedom and fullness God intends for us is the scarcity mindset. We are powerful divine beings with unlimited potential and resources to support us in fulfilling our destiny. But we choose to live like paupers, instead of the princes and princesses that we really are.

In the beginning, when Adam and Eve bought into the lie in the Garden of Eden, shame and fear entered their heart and warped their perspective of who they were and who God is. They learned new patterns of coping and behaving from an orphan mindset instead of as sons and daughters. We, too, have inherited an orphan spirit, and our experiences have created a disconnect that keeps us stuck in the belief that there's never enough. There's never enough time, money, resources, or support. Again, we believe that old lie that we can't trust God's love or His provision.

We feel that we are on our own, and we will have to go without, so we must make things happen for ourselves. So, we strive and struggle to get what we can. As a result of this mindset, we feel slighted.

We tell ourselves things like, "I have to work harder to get half of what everybody else does." "What I need and want isn't available to me." "To have that, I have to sacrifice this." "I can't trust God to fill in my gaps. I have to fill them in for myself." "I have to keep doing what makes me miserable because I have no other choice." "I have to work harder and longer to create more success for myself."

The scarcity mindset also convinces us that when we see someone else receive a blessing, it takes away from the provision that could be ours–that someone else's blessing costs us our own. This mindset wrecked me for years. I lived in constant paralyzing fear and doubt that I wouldn't have what I wanted and needed. I was fearful of going without and of missing out, so I lived unclear, unfocused, and unaligned with the real me. I settled and struggled in every area of my life.

We may have fallen prey to the scarcity mindset because of disappointment and lack in our lives that caused us to believe lies about ourselves and God. We may have learned it from our parents. No matter how it started, we must decide to break the poverty mindset's stronghold by receiving from God the revelation of our true identity and inheritance. We must also be willing to reprogram our thoughts with God's truth, the abundance mindset, until our beliefs are transformed. Then we can live as victors, not victims, as sons and daughters, not as orphans.

Shifting into an abundance mindset is a daily choice for each of us. It requires us to cultivate a trust in the creative energy and flow of the universe as God created it. John 10:10, says, "I have come to give you everything in abundance, more than you expect–life in its fullness until you overflow!" (TPT). We must focus on where we already have more than enough and trust that there is always more available to us.

When we focus on lack, we close off possibility. We think negative thoughts and make judgments that reinforce lack and fear. We have to stop buying into that lie and start trading fear and lack for faith that more is always available. The truth is that resources are always flowing to us in abundance like a river. When we are open to receive it, the new flows in when we need it, and the things that are no longer serving us flow out.

Abundance and prosperity are our inheritance. Promise land-living is our birthright, and as Warriors, we must claim ownership and step into what is ours to possess.

POWERLESSNESS

The final mental stronghold that hinders us from unleashing our greatness and living our best life is powerlessness. We are mighty, divine Warriors, but we often choose to live powerlessly.

From a young age, we learn what standards and expectations we must live up to and what roles we must play in our families, and we carry those out throughout our lives. We perform and people please to gain approval and acceptance, and we live on autopilot in the same patterns that we've always known. We don't stop to examine where those patterns are leading us. Many of us never learn how to take ownership of our choices and decisions.

Further, in our painful experiences, disappointment, and delay discourage us. Over time, we develop a defeated mindset, and we operate out of it.

We believe, "I can't do or have what I want." "I can't be myself." "I have to keep doing this because if I don't, there will be retribution." "I have to stay in this relationship because I'm stuck." We believe we are powerless to change anything even though we are struggling and miserable.

During my personal coaching journey, I heard many of these statements come out of my mouth frequently. I couldn't make that change. I couldn't do what I wanted to do. I had to keep seeing that many clients. I had to keep tolerating that person's behavior in my life. I couldn't say what I really thought and how I felt. I had to keep doing what others expected of me. What I really wanted wasn't going to happen for me. As long as I believed those lies, I lived in frustration and desperation.

Soon, I realized that I had felt powerless for as long as I could remember. It seemed that everybody else was much more powerful than me. They could make changes and choices. Living with this belief was overwhelming and scary. I felt like a prisoner in my own life.

Then, my conviction eventually turned into hope. If I start thinking and living like the mighty Warrior that I am, what would that look like?

That would mean that I would gain clarity about what I really wanted and what mattered most to me and start living in alignment with it. I could live out the passion and purpose that God wired in me and stop living for the acceptance and approval of others. I could disappoint people. I could decide when I wanted to say "yes" and "no." I could set healthy boundaries. I could do more of what I love and less of what I didn't. I didn't have to keep tolerating what wasn't best for me. I could start believing that "I can…" and "I will…" instead of "I can't…" and "it won't…" Instead of "I have to…" I could believe "I choose to…" and "I get to…"

I realized that I needed to repent from a life of powerlessness, and to do that, I must identify the lies I believed and break agreement with them. As I did, it was clear how they had kept me stuck for far too long. It was a huge step toward freedom.

I made this declaration daily:

"I am a powerful, divine Warrior, and I make powerfully positive changes in my life that align with my passions and purpose. I trust that I am chosen, loved, and highly favored, and have perfect wisdom for each step in my journey."

Not only did I change my mindset, but I began to take courageous action to make more decisions that aligned with my passions, my priorities, and my purpose. Little by little, I took back my life.

Taking powerful action was a game-changer, and I am now passionate about empowering and equipping others with its transformational truth.

Maybe life doesn't look like you thought it would at this point. You may feel like what you really want will never happen for you. You may be asking yourself what you did wrong. Perhaps you're beating yourself up because you don't have it all figured out.

When we stay focused on our circumstances, we feel frustrated, discouraged, and disappointed–even depressed. What if instead of focusing on our current life conditions, we become inspired by our calling?

We are most powerful when we live our truth, living out of our most authentic selves and honoring our hearts. When we don't feel powerful, it is because we are living or believing a lie–about ourselves, about God, or about what is available to us, and it steals the power of who we were created to be.

Along the way, we disconnect from the power of our inner Warrior. Yet, when we are empowered with truth, our inner Warrior awakens and arises into his or her greatness. We can bravely, freely, and authentically thrive in the life of freedom and fullness that is already ours!

Our dreams call us into the more God intended for us. He placed these dreams in us, and He wants to manifest them in and through us. However, we can't fulfill our calling or manifest our vision when we focus on what is. We must focus on what we can't see.

We can't remain in the right now or even in our yesterdays. We must look to the hope of our future. Allow that hope to energize and inspire you. Let God's power move in you, expanding your capacity to receive the more He has for you.

Listen to, focus on, believe in that calling inside of you that burns brighter and is much more powerful than anything else. Follow it to the destiny that is waiting for you.

REFLECTION

"No weapon forged against you will prevail, and you will
refute every tongue that accuses you. This is the heritage
of the servants of the Lord, and this is their
vindication from me, declares the Lord."

—Isaiah 54:7 *(NIV)*

What does living your best self and your best life look like to you? Get out your paper and pen and describe your dream life.

As you review this, what messages of doubt, fear, or shame bombard your mind with loud, intrusive thoughts and accusations?

Are there areas in your life where you feel stuck? What lies are you believing that are keeping you there? Ask God to reveal the strongholds that are holding the lie in place.

What does the voice of doubt tell you? How does it limit you?

How does the voice of fear bully you? How is fear keeping you out of the more that God has for you?

What lies does shame whisper to you? How do you respond? What is shame stealing from you?

Do you have a scarcity mindset? How? What lies are you believing that give it power?

Are you living powerlessly? What powerless thoughts do you have and beliefs? How would life change for you if you began to live powerfully?

APPLICATION

"Never doubt God's mighty power to work in you and accomplish all this. He will achieve infinite more than your greatest request, your most unbelievable dream, and exceed your wildest imagination. He will outdo them all, for His miraculous power constantly energizes you."

—Ephesians 3:20 (*THE MIRROR*)

Are you caught up in your current life conditions rather than being inspired by your calling?

What is calling to you in the deepest part of you?

What is that passion in you that burns so brightly?

What is the dream inside of you that is your destiny?

Let God's power move in you and expand your capacity to receive the more He has for you.

Stop listening to the voice of fear and self-doubt. Stop listening to the lies that keep you stuck in the limits of what you can see. There is so much more.

Listen to, focus on, believe in that calling inside of you that burns brighter and is much more powerful than anything else. Follow it to the more that is intended on you–the destiny that is waiting for you.

CHAPTER FIFTEEN

Behavioral Pitfalls

"My dilemma is that even though I sincerely desire to do that
which is good, I don't, and the things I despise, I do."

—Romans 7:15b *(NIV)*

GETTING VICTORY OVER OUR MENTAL strongholds is a step into our best selves and our best life. After we unravel the lies we have believed that have kept us in bondage, we also must transform our comfortable old habits and limiting behavioral patterns. It's important that we examine our lives for things that no longer work for us. We need to take an honest look at what needs to change to move us closer to the desires of our hearts.

Does your lifestyle consistently exceed your budget? Do your impulsive spending habits prevent you from saving for your future?

Do you live reactively because you never take the time to prioritize and schedule how you will spend your time and energy? Are you tired of not having enough of either for what is most important to you? Perhaps you live in overwhelm because you fear missing out, you struggle with saying no, or you haven't clarified what you really want.

Do you keep saying you'll go to bed earlier but continue to eat late, check out in front of the TV, or scroll through social media again? Maybe you say you're going to eat healthier but fail to plan meals, continuing to grab fast food and make poor choices.

Do you crave a deeper connection with your spouse, but offer everybody else the best of you so that he or she only gets the leftovers?

Do you drink that third or fourth glass of alcohol at night convincing yourself that it's the only thing that helps you relax?

Let's face the truth. Our bad habits are simply patterns of behavior that we use to cope with being uncomfortable. Though they offer relief or instantaneous gratification, they keep us stuck in a place we don't really want to be. To change our behavioral patterns and transform our lives, we must become aware of what we're doing and why. Then, we must interrupt and replace the pattern with a more effective one that will offer us what we are truly craving.

We need to take an honest look at how we live and ask ourselves what needs to change to move us closer to the desires of our hearts and the life that God intended. Which behaviors hinder us from experiencing the transformation we genuinely want? Think about your familiar and automatic daily routines and practices. Where are they leading you?

Many of us live every day at our current capacity. We don't realize that to carry the more that is available to us, we have to expand our capacity. This was true for me, too. Although disciplined in doing inner work daily, I didn't understand that this was a prerequisite for growth. We have to expand our capacity to move to the next level. It is like strength training. We have to get stronger so that we can carry more.

I was programmed to be disciplined, to have good habits, and I had continued them fairly consistently in some areas of life. Yet, living the life I dreamed of living required me to make significant adjustments. As I examined my routines and habits, I realized that there were major gaps in several areas.

I needed to work on the way I viewed, valued, and managed money. I needed to take responsibility for my health by moderating my eating and exercise habits. I needed to work on connecting deeper in my relationships and in my spiritual life. I needed to firm up my boundaries, and balance how I spent my time and energy. I needed to restructure how I managed and marketed my business and stop tolerating things I wasn't okay with or that were no longer serving me. I also needed to learn how to do less and receive more. It was time for some serious change.

With the help of my life coach, counselor, and several other professional resources, I grew and developed myself personally and professionally to make those necessary changes to level up my life and my business. Yet, in addition to the individual habits that were hindering my growth in several specific areas of my life, a few more pervasive patterns that I call behavioral pitfalls were immobilizing me.

In almost two decades of professional counseling and coaching, I've watched these same traps enslave hundreds of others in the bondage of a same-old stuck, small existence. It's time that we recognize how we are being imprisoned by them and robbed of the life God intended for us.

It's crucial that we understand that our behavior patterns may have worked for us for a long time, but they won't take us from surviving to thriving. Let's explore several of the common behavioral pitfalls that ensnare us and learn what it takes to break free from their oppression.

LIVING SOMEONE ELSE'S STORY

The first pitfall that keeps people stuck is trying to live in someone else's story. There is nothing more stressful, overwhelming, or exhausting than trying to be someone else or someone else's idea of who we should be. So often, we find ourselves living according to our "shoulds," our expectations, and our fantasies.

We strive to be someone other than who we are and crave a life that is not ours to live. When we fall prey to this habit, we live in confusion and turmoil about who we need to be, how we need to show up, and what we need to do to make it happen. We typically do what we see others doing, or we follow a strategy or formula that we read in a book somewhere or heard from someone we respect. We are frustrated when it doesn't work out for us the way it has for someone else. And we are left feeling defeated, like a failure, when our life doesn't measure up to our idealized picture.

I spent most of my life living this way. I wanted to be someone else. I thought everyone else had it all figured out. I assumed they were happy and that if I looked the part, if I achieved what they did and became who they were, then I would finally be okay. So I didn't show up as me. I was so busy trying to live someone else's story, I couldn't be happy or live powerfully in my own.

Let me save you some time.

Be you.

Stop comparing. Stop idealizing other people's lives and rejecting your own. Stop researching what other people are doing. Stop following formulas and strategies that frustrate and drain you. Clear out what isn't you and what is not serving you. Stop buying into the destination addiction trap of "I'll be happy when…" Stop denying your heart and your truth.

Stop living someone else's life. Start living by what really matters to you.

Only you can play the irreplaceable role in the beautiful story God is writing for you. It is the privilege of a lifetime.

DISTRACTIONS

The second pitfall that ensnares us in unproductive patterns of behavior is distraction. This is one of the greatest weapons of our enemy. Distractions constantly lure our hearts and minds away from our purpose. Several of the distractions that enticed me were other people's opinions, other people's drama, fear of missing out, self-doubt, a cluttered mind, an overloaded schedule, burdens that weren't mine to carry, and chaos.

I allowed everybody else to dictate how I lived by saying "yes" to projects, obligations, and potential opportunities that did not align with my passion or purpose. As a result, I had to say "no" to myself all too often. I had no idea how much time and energy I lost on a daily basis because I didn't know how to own my life.

Perhaps you struggle with some of the same distractions I did, or maybe the challenges that divert you are different. No matter how varied our distractions are, we must be willing to see the truth about what they are stealing from us. Otherwise, we will never be able to free ourselves from their trap. When I awakened to the reality of what the distractions in my life were stealing from me–my identity, my deepest desires, my true purpose, meaningful relationships, along with freedom, peace, and fulfillment–I stopped being so mad with myself and started getting angry at the enemy's deceptive tactics.

My outrage empowered me to eliminate the chaos that was cheating me out of the fullness of life God promises. I began to spend my time, energy, and resources intently focused on and aligned with the life I wanted to be living and the work that I really wanted to be doing.

Working with my coach and counselor, I clarified what is most important to me. I reconnected with my values and priorities. I learned to listen to my heart and discern what was best for me in each situation. Instead of overfilling my days, I said "no" to what is not meant for me, to anything that felt heavy or forced. Simplifying my life gave me the freedom and margin to say "yes" to my destiny.

The more I starved my distractions and fed my focus, the more I understood how crucial it is to set firm and healthy boundaries with others. Instead of worrying about what everybody else needed, wanted, or expected from me, I chose to live the life I wanted to live and do the work I was passionate about doing. I let go of people-pleasing, approval-seeking, carrying burdens, being overly responsible, and fearing missing out.

Even Jesus, the greatest, most compassionate servant who ever lived, never responded out of obligation, expectation, approval, or even in response to someone's need. Instead, He listened intently to the voice of His Father and went where the Father sent Him. When He met a need, it was out of the overflow of what God poured into Him. He honored His need for rest, refueling, and rejuvenation by retreating away from the crowds.

Breaking life-long habits takes commitment, discipline, time, and effort, but it is worth it. It's not easy, and it's definitely more about progress than perfection. Some days, I am still lured away by shiny objects, and occasionally, I fall into an old familiar trap. But when I realize what has happened, I quickly remember that I am opposed by an enemy who is threatened by the powerful Warrior that I am and who will do anything to keep from me living in my destiny. I regroup by reminding myself of who I am, what my purpose is, what is most important to me, and the life of freedom and fullness that I am fighting for. And I know that victory is mine.

FORCING THINGS TO HAPPEN

The third pitfall that keeps us stuck in ineffective habits is choosing to live in force versus flow. So often, we try to force things to happen in our lives that aren't in alignment with our purpose or that are outside of

God's plan or timing for us. When we do, it takes a toll on our mental, physical, and spiritual health.

When we are trying to force something, our body's energy becomes heavy and dense. The life force energy that God breathes into us begins to fade, and if we are present and aware, it will feel like our energy is stuck and stagnant. I have experienced this feeling many times in seasons where my life was unbalanced and chaotic. It happens every time I decide to move ahead of God or make something happen for myself rather than trust God's plan or wait for His perfect timing.

What often accompanies this pattern of striving and stress is minimal physical or emotional release–lack of adequate rest, exercise, and nourishment for my body or my spirit. Everything in my head gets noisy, and my schedule gets overloaded. My creativity is blocked, and I stop hearing from God.

I used to stay in this place for much longer than I do now. As I tried to force my will on my circumstances, joy and peace eluded me. In frustration and turmoil, I wondered, "What is wrong with me? Why isn't this happening for me the way I want and need it to?"

Now I understand that when I am forcing my will and way in life, I am blocking the Holy Spirit's flow in me. I don't want to spend any more time or energy driven by fear or striving for success. That way of surviving is fruitless and futile. I want to live Spirit-led in every moment, attuned to the wisest Counselor there is. I want to live passion-fueled and purpose-centered, trusting and abiding in God's beautiful plan and perfect timing. When I live in flow from a place of rest and receiving, the fruit of my life is sweet.

A few years ago, I heard God whisper the words, "life force energy" into my spirit.

"Tune in, and let my life force flow from you," He said. "It's the force. It's YOUR force."

His words reminded me of the scene with Yoda and Luke Skywalker in the Empire Strikes Back. I smiled as truth resonated in my spirit. I felt that familiar tingly feeling run up my spine, the one I get when I know God is speaking truth into my core. Deep peace washed over me.

God is the source of our life force energy. He breathed life into us from the very first breath we took, and His Spirit continues to flow through us every day. But when we aren't aligned with His flow of energy, our soul, spirit, and body start to die a slow death. We desperately need His life force flowing through us at all times. Any other way is not really living–it is existing.

Make the decision today to stop battling yourself and stop resisting the Spirit's flow of life in you by trying to force your will on your circumstances. Instead, learn how to tune in to your heart, to the flow of the Spirit within you and open to receive all the good there is for you. This is your greatest source of support and wisdom. From this place, you receive supernatural strength and courage, too. It is the source of healing, peace, joy, and abundance. In the beautiful, harmonious flow of His Spirit, you will experience transformation from the inside out. Your life will never be the same again. You'll live with more freedom and fullness than you can imagine.

LIVING INCONGRUENTLY

Living incongruently is the fourth common pitfall that caps our capacity to grow. I learned this concept from a counselor and coach, Ken Edwards, who is quick to note when I'm not living according to my truth. He doesn't hesitate to firmly but lovingly say so and has called me out many times when he observed a choice or an action in my life that didn't align with who I really am, what I say is most important to me, or my purpose.

One time in particular, I was making an important decision about the direction I wanted to grow my business. I was excited about the potential of an opportunity that stroked my ego. It lured me in hard and fast, but before it swallowed me up, Ken reminded me that it was incongruent with my desire for more freedom. Though it looked like an opportunity to expand and grow to the next level, it almost certainly would lead to more bondage for me. I'm so grateful that his gentle guidance directed me to make wise choices that were congruent with my deepest desires.

My commitment to living authentically and congruently has enhanced my life and my business in impactful ways. Now, when there is a choice to be made, I simply ask myself, "Is this me?" The answer is usually very clear.

When my life gets stressful and unbalanced, I know to take a time out. I look for what I've taken on or what I've gotten involved in that doesn't fit. With this clarity, I can reclaim my peace.

If your life feels stressful and unbalanced, it's time to take an honest look at how you may be living incongruently. What feels heavy or burdensome, even though it may be a good opportunity? Maybe it's great for someone else, but it's not best for you. Perhaps it's not for you in this season of life.

Are there decisions you've made that don't align with who you are and what you say matters most to you? Maybe you're spending time and energy on something that you're good at or that you enjoy, but at this point, it's a detour from your true passion and purpose. If so, don't allow shame or obligation to divert you even more.

You're never stuck. You can make a change in your life anytime. Simply realign your heart with truth. Reroute your path. Make a U-turn when needed, and get back on course.

LIVING CONDITIONALLY

The fifth common pitfall that hinders our growth is living conditionally. We live conditionally when we wait for all the good things in our lives to show up and our circumstances to be aligned with what we think should be BEFORE we feel gratitude.

I spent over forty years living this way, and I experienced perpetual frustration and discontentment. Until I awakened to the fact that this way of living is backwards, I stayed stuck and stagnant. When I discovered the power that gratitude unlocks in us, I knew it was one of the most important habits I could cultivate.

Gratitude is an emotional state we choose to live in. Implementing a daily practice of gratitude shifts our mindset and accelerates our frequency, which naturally and miraculously opens us up to all of the possibilities of the greater and more that is available.

Instead of focusing on what we don't have, which is the way most people live, we must practice focusing on what we do have. We have to train our mind to not just appreciate the good in life but also to be grateful for what we know is coming.

Yet, there is another level of gratitude that I have learned and experienced, and I challenge you to learn to live here, too. It is choosing to shift your perspective to seeing any problem or struggle that happens in your life as something that is happening FOR you and not TO you! This takes courage and intentional practice but making this a habit has been a game changer for me!

It requires that when something we want doesn't happen for us, we choose to feel gratitude for it because we see it as contrast instead of loss or lack. The truth is that it is simply a contrast from what we think we wanted, but there is something better and greater that is available to us and on its way. Contrast creates clarity for us. We have to let go of what we are grasping so tightly to allow the new and greater in. The new can't come in without us creating white space in our lives for it to appear.

I challenge you to begin leveling up your gratitude practice by no longer viewing anything as bad or wrong. See everything as an opportunity for you to grow, expand, and level up. Haven't your biggest breakthroughs always come from your greatest breakdowns? I know mine have. So, how we choose to look at a situation and respond to it determines what is possible for us.

The only thing we can be certain of is that life is constantly changing, and we can't choose to focus on and act on the losses and failures. There are no losses and failures if we don't judge them as such. The fact is that true transformation is a process of letting go of what is and opening up to the more and better. To receive what's next, we can't be afraid of letting go of what we have. If we do, we are choosing to operate from lack and fear. The degree to which we are able to let go is the degree to which we are opening to receive the new to come into our lives.

When I began to understand this concept and practice new levels of gratitude as a way of being, my life leveled up in major ways. I now choose to see everything from the perspective that I am lucky and blessed no matter what. I don't see loss or lack anymore. I see only gain.

Training my mind to focus on what this current situation or circumstance is preparing me for, how it is expanding me, and what is now becoming possible for me has unlocked joy and abundance in my heart, mind, and life that I never could have imagined.

It's time to level up your living. I challenge you to implement this gratitude practice in your life. Stop waiting on your life conditions to change before you feel grateful and blessed. If you are intentional about cultivating a daily habit of gratitude, you shift into living in a constant state of receiving. The more and the greater will flow in and astound you. When you live unconditionally in a consistent state of gratitude, you will feel happier and healthier, and every area of your life will be powerfully transformed in amazing ways.

Warriors battle for what matters most to their hearts. We are willing to suffer for what we love. We learned many of our patterns of behavior out of our need to survive and never stopped to question their effectiveness.

Living a passion-fueled and purpose-centered life requires discipline. We are what we repeatedly do. Big results come from actions we take regularly. Small, consistent steps add up to big changes.

We can choose to stop running on autopilot and settling for instant gratification. We can break out of the comfortable and familiar. We can take full ownership and personal responsibility for our behaviors by eliminating our excuses. Breaking up with habits we've been cozy with for years or even decades may feel painful. Yet, the pain of change is nothing compared to the pain of regret.

Being yourself, saying no, living congruently, in flow, may feel like moving to a foreign land. When it seems unbearable, when you're weary and ready to give up, remember this:

That discomfort you feel is the catalyst that will move you toward the freedom and fulfillment you yearn for. Rather than trying so hard to stop doing something, focus instead on starting something new. Shift the energy drain from tired old behaviors into new routines and exciting adventures.

When you make this change, you'll have open space, time, and energy to discover what will permanently fill the ache inside. Solutions will emerge, and the path before you will lead you to a new life.

REFLECTION

*"When Jesus saw him lying there and learned that he
had been in this condition for a long time, he asked him,
"Do you want to get well?"*

—John 5:6 *(NIV)*

What habits, behaviors, or choices are preventing you from developing, growing, and expanding? What are you tired of feeling? What are you sick of tolerating?

How is it working for you to continue walking down that well-worn path instead of dealing with the real feeling you keep avoiding?

What is it that you're avoiding that you need to face once and for all?

How are you staying stuck because you're trying to live in someone else's story? How are you trying to live according to "shoulds," expectations, or a fantasy?

What distractions lure you away from your purpose and the life God intended for you?

How are you living in force versus flow? How are you being driven by fear or striving for success instead of living Spirit-led, passion-fueled, and purpose-centered?

Are you resisting the more that God has for you because you are resisting more than receiving? What needs to shift? Will you trade your "no" for a big "yes" and be open to receive what's next?

How are you living incongruently to who you are and with what matters most to you?

Are you living conditionally? How is that perpetuating frustration and keeping you stuck? Are you committed to cultivate a daily practice of next level gratitude? How will implementing that practice change your life for the better?

How would your life change if you began to see everything as happening FOR you instead of TO you?

What one or two habits, if you change them, will alter the trajectory of your life? Your work? Your business? Your health? Your relationships? Your finances? Your happiness?

APPLICATION

*"As you yield freely and fully to the dynamic life and power
of the Holy Spirit, you will abandon the cravings of your
self-life. For your self-life craves the things that offend the
Holy Spirit and hinder him from living free within you! And
the Holy Spirit's intense cravings hinder your old self-life
from dominating you! So then, the two incompatible
and conflicting forces within you are your self-life of
the flesh and the new creation life of the Spirit."*

—Galatians 5:16-17 *(TPT)*

Get honest with yourself about why you're living the way you are. Examine the habits that are keeping you stuck in survival when you were made to thrive.

Interrupt your same old patterns with healthier, more effective ones. Even if it feels right. Even if it feels comfortable and familiar. Even if it's all you've ever known. Take an honest look right now, and see what needs to change.

Instead of dreading the overwhelming work that drains your energy, spend more time and energy every week doing things you enjoy.

Instead of grabbing that sweet treat, acknowledge your true hunger, nourish your body or soul with the rest or the fuel you need. Choose healthier foods that fuel your body in more efficient ways.

Rather than spending money on clothes, shoes, homes, or cars to fill the emptiness, begin saving even small amounts of your money so you can enjoy financial freedom and peace.

Exchange that third glass of wine with an honest conversation with your spouse, acknowledging your true feelings.

Instead of hitting snooze again, alleviate the things that exhaust or overwhelm you. Connect with those who support you and talk about what causes you stress.

Rather than buying another thing you don't need, do more things that interest and fulfill you.

Instead of playing the performance or approval game at the expense of your health and happiness, listen to and honor what you need and want in each moment.

Expose bad habits for what they really are—counterfeit. Stop escaping from your reality and start honoring your deeper yearning with what is truly satisfying.

Step out of your existence and into a more fulfilling life. It's available and merely waiting for you to choose it.

When you feel heavy and blocked, learn to tune into, trust, and enhance God's flow of life force energy within. Soon, you will feel more alive, connected, and healthier in every way.

Tap into the most powerful Life Force in the universe. His power, His peace, and His flow matched with your true essence, your divine purpose, and your Warrior mindsets and habits are a winning combination.

CHAPTER SIXTEEN

Warrior Arise!

*"Arise, shine, for your light has come, and the glory
of the Lord has risen upon you."*

—Isaiah 60:1 *(ESV)*

MARK TWAIN SAID, "The two most important days in your life
are the day you were born and the day you find out why."

Discovering my "why" changed everything for me. It brought
me hope and a sense of value and significance. After so many disappointments, perceived failures, and then a breakdown of my mental,
emotional, and physical health, I was desperate for healing, freedom,
and life transformation.

When I exchanged a lifetime of lies for a life aligned with my gifts,
values, strengths, and passions, my purpose became clear. I realized
that my heart is the center of my passion and power. It is my seat of
wisdom, and when I am connected to it, I hear God's voice and discern
His truth. This clarity now guides every decision I make, whether
personal or business. Every day, I understand more clearly that living

in the truth of who we really are is the key to thriving in true freedom and fulfillment.

Knowing my "why" also helped me understand why I had struggled so much up to that point in my life. It made everything I had been through worth the pain and loss I experienced. It gave me hope and freedom I had never felt and inspired me to move forward boldly and bravely into the next chapter in my life and work.

When we live in our true identity, we can understand our purpose. This knowledge guides our path and fuels everything we do. When we are doing what God created us to do, He abundantly provides everything we need to accomplish our goals. Knowing what we are here for helps us make daily decisions about how to spend our time, energy, and resources. Purpose replaces distraction, chaos, and overwhelm with a compass, which keeps us on course.

THE POWER OF PURPOSE

Each of us has God-given gifts and strengths. Like superheroes, we were created with special powers and a heart for a unique purpose.

Proverbs 18:6 promises, "A man's gift makes room for him, and brings him before the great." *(ESV)*

Every great man and woman in the Bible was a Warrior. Scripture is full of references to Warriors. It's paramount that we hear and believe God's truth on this critical topic.

First, we must understand that God, Himself, is a Warrior. "The Lord is a Warrior; the Lord is His name." —Exodus 15:3 *(NIV)*

"The LORD your God is with you, the Mighty Warrior who saves. He will take great delight in you; in His love he will no longer rebuke you, but will rejoice over you with singing." —Zephaniah 3:17 *(NIV)*

If God is a Warrior, and we are His children, then we are Warriors too.

When the angel of the Lord appeared to Gideon, he said, "The Lord is with you, mighty Warrior." —Judges 6:12 (NIV)

In Ephesians 6, Paul commands Christians to "Put on the full armor of God, so you can take your stand against the devil's schemes."

In Revelation 19, Jesus returns as a warrior riding a white horse, wearing His blood-stained robe, leading a mighty army with a sword.

A Warrior is a person who stands firmly in who they are and who battles fiercely against all threats for what they hold dear. A Warrior says, "This is who I am. This is my family. This is my faith. This is my God. This is my purpose. This is my destiny. This is my heart. These are my beliefs."

To an enemy, a Warrior says, "You will not hurt me or take what I love without coming through me."

Every great Warrior knows first and foremost who they are and what their purpose is. They live confidently in their unique strengths and passions that enable them to fulfill that special purpose. Unleashed, we make an irreplaceable imprint and impact on the world. Our footprint is like no other. No one can do what we were born to do.

MISSION TO FREEDOM

For many years, I lived with a big disconnect that created intense feelings of frustration and, in many moments, sheer hopelessness. The Bible said that as a follower of Jesus, I was free from sin, created to live a life of freedom and abundance. Yet, I lived in bondage and poverty.

Then, more and more, I saw the same disconnect in the lives of the clients I counseled. I realized that they, too, wanted to live the life God promised, but instead, they felt stuck and powerless in their struggle and existence. I knew God's promises were true, so there must be something I was missing. It wasn't enough for me to manage my life anymore, and I didn't want to help others merely manage theirs either.

I wanted to live as the victor that God said I was, and I wanted to help those that God called me to help to live victoriously, too.

As a life and success coach of hundreds of men and women, time and time again, I see that what keeps most people from reaching the success and impact they deeply desire is lack of a reservoir of powerful courage and positive energy to move to the next level. They get comfortable. They settle in and sleep-walk through most of their life, stuck in responsibility, duty, and obligation. They live there cozily unless something forces them out of that space, like the kind of awakening that happened to me.

So, I made it my mission to discover the solution to closing the gap so I could get the breakthrough I was seeking and guide my clients to do the same.

MY WARRIOR JOURNEY

Having battled my counterfeit warrior, Strong Connie, for most of my life, I knew that I could be fierce and strong. My Warrior training really began when I was ready to leave behind the misery, torment, and the wake of destruction this counterfeit warrior caused in my life. As I progressed, life and hope began to rise up in the Warrior that God created me to be. I was determined to allow God to cultivate and empower her as she awakened inside.

With my coach and therapists' help, I dove full force into my own personal and professional development work over the next several years. At the same time, I studied every resource I could find to grow and develop my inner Warrior.

At the beginning of this process, no area in my life was where I wanted it to be. I was overwhelmed with all that needed to change. Kami reminded me throughout our work together that this is a process, not a destination. Ken would encourage me that it is a journey of becoming. They both promised that the more I showed up ready to receive life-transforming truth and new information, the more progress I would make. So, I committed to them and to myself that I would show up fully, honestly, and vulnerably, ready to see with new eyes and receive new wisdom with a heart wide open.

Reconnecting to my heart, passion, and values and discovering my true essence and purpose transformed me. As my perspective changed, patterns of ineffective thinking and behaving were uprooted. My life and work shifted and expanded in amazing ways. The awakening experience ignited my inner fire, and my hope for the More that God has for me was renewed.

Everything got better. As I settled into changes in my life and work, I felt happier and more fulfilled than I ever had before. I woke up energized and inspired. My days were filled with joy. I was excited about my future. God introduced me to new friends and blessed me with a loving, supportive community of like-minded and hearted people I love and enjoy life with.

He also brought a Godly man into my life who has a heart like His. He sees me, understands me, and loves me for me. It's taken me some time to comprehend and receive it, but I'm learning. God is lovingly teaching me how to be a woman and be loved, protected, and cared for even though I am strong and independent. The Lord is my Savior and my provider, so now He is freeing my heart to love and enjoy a man rather than need or worship one.

People ask me all the time why I'm not yet married. At this point, I love my life so much that it's not my top priority. I no longer need someone else to make me feel whole and complete. Needing a partner and desiring one is very different. God placed a desire in my heart to be married to the love of my life, my soul mate. I still have the dream of bringing my heart and my life together with that like-minded and like-hearted man God has for me, and building something beautiful together for His glory. When it's time, my heart will know.

As my business grew, other therapists and coaches sought me out to work with me. My practice expanded into a group practice, and our influence and impact in our community multiplied. Coaching clients found me. Opportunities to serve and lead in our community emerged as well as invitations for speaking engagements. I was also asked by several other leaders in the personal and professional development industry to collaborate in new endeavors that positively impacted people's lives.

God placed several gifted Kingdom-minded people in my life to advise, teach, love, and guide me. One of those was a friend of a friend, Linda, who helped me seek clarity from God about vision for my ministry. During one of our collaborative prayer sessions, Linda heard the word "Arise!" Immediately, we studied the meaning of the word in Hebrew, and discovered that "arise" means to stand, to be established, to become powerful, and to come on the scene. I knew right away that this was a prophetic word from the Lord to me.

Two days later, I was given a book about the story of Deborah, who was a prophetess and a judge in Israel. In the book of Judges, Deborah sent a message to the nation's military leaders to form an army to battle the Canaanites, who had oppressed them for many years. They were victorious, as God had told her they would be, and peace came to the land.

"… I, Deborah, arose as a mother in Israel." —Judges 5:7 *(ESV)*

This story and this word birthed a vision in me to lead a movement of men and women–fire starters, truth seekers, change-makers, and trailblazers–who will Arise to be the Warriors they were created to be. They will live in the fullness of their true identity and in the power of their purpose and destiny.

It hasn't been easy though. Greater impact, influence, and exposure led to more enemy attacks. A brutal but beautiful pruning process led to incredible growth and maturity, sharpening my ability to lead and develop the business. I've learned some tough lessons about loving, pouring into, and managing people. I know more now about showing up fully, authentically, and vulnerably while leading something bigger than me, something for Kingdom purposes and not for my own achievement or glory. Learning and healing took place simultaneously in God's Warrior boot camp. It was hard but worth all the tears, sweat, and hardships.

Through every struggle, battle, and opposition, I firmly stoked the fire that burned brightly in me. I trusted my Warrior within, and God shaped the "What's Next" for me around that faith. What an incredible growth experience it has been!

NO GOING BACK

Looking back now, I'm grateful that the circumstances of my life didn't work out for me. I'm thankful that my body began to shut down. Otherwise, I may have continued struggling, striving, and surviving for many more years.

Thank God, there was no going back for me. Had I not fully and courageously embraced this inner work, I would have continued living a small, self-focused, and limited existence.

God has so much more planned for each of us than we can think, dream, or imagine (Ephesians 3:20). It's not just for me, but for you, too—a unique, special, incredible destiny for you to fulfill that is all yours.

My hope and challenge are for you to commit to doing your inner work and discovering the destiny that is waiting for you. When we live in the center of our true essence, and in our passion and purpose, we are our most authentic, most powerful, and most fulfilled self. Any other way of living is merely existing and surviving.

Why would we choose to continue living that way? God assures us that we have a promised land to inhabit, an inheritance that is all ours to possess, and a full and free life waiting for us to claim and step into it. We must be willing to open to the "more" to awaken our Warrior within. We must fully embrace and engage in the discipline and training that will enable us to become our most authentic and powerful self. Then we can live victoriously over all that hinders us from stepping into our greatness.

THE WARRIOR'S HEART

Unfortunately, often the first thing we tune out when we experience pain and struggle is our heart. We buy into the lie that our hearts can't be trusted, and therefore we disconnect from our true selves and from God. We move from really living to merely existing, doing what we think we have to do to make life work for us. We forfeit our superpowers, locking ourselves in a prison of performance and addictions to fill the ache created by a fake existence.

I believe the greatest battle facing a Warrior is the fight for our own heart. Evil and brokenness in this world threaten our ability to show up fully, freely, wholeheartedly, and authentically. Our true identity and destiny are often casualties on this spiritual battlefield. We must awaken to the truth and then empower and equip our Warrior within to defeat our opposition with wisdom, courage, and fierceness. Our freedom depends on it.

Fortunately, God supernaturally battles alongside us. When we are free, we connect and commune with Him personally and intimately and claim our inheritance as His beloved children. The power of His presence and the truth of His Word remove all hindrances and tear down all strongholds. When we are free, we help our fellow brothers and sisters escape the deceptive bondage of this world, thereby advancing God's Kingdom on Earth.

MY GOD STORY

I was the girl who didn't want her story. I wanted my brother's story. I wanted the story of the NFL quarterback's wife. I wanted the story of the fitness model or the national best-selling author. I wanted the glory because I needed so badly to be noticed and to be valuable.

But God loves me so much that He wasn't going to give me something that wasn't going to fill my most authentic longing–that was just going to leave me more starved and desperate than ever before. He wasn't going to give me the counterfeit of fame and more achievement. He would not allow me to continue to prove myself over and over when what I really wanted was to feel safe and secure and intimately known and loved–not admired by acquaintances or approved of for my performance.

I am not a better writer of my story than my Creator, who loves me beyond what I can comprehend. He writes the most beautiful stories. He gives us life that satisfies our heart's deepest longings, even those we have forgotten or buried under our shame or the rubble of others' expectations.

I've learned the hard way that nothing we can get for ourselves will fulfill us. This is one of the greatest lies the devil wants us to believe. There is not a person you meet, a thing you acquire, an achievement you master, or a circumstance that happens that will finally fill the longing of your heart. No status you attain in your personal or professional life, no place where you arrive, no amount of money you make will create a place of lasting contentment for you.

We are created with a God-sized hole that cannot be satisfied with anything other than a personal, deep, intimate relationship with Him.

Today, my life is much more fulfilling. My relationships are deeper. I see beauty again. I appreciate silliness, and I laugh a lot more. I am learning to be present and feel connected. I allow myself to be loved.

I've realized that life and love were available to me when I was willing to open to it, allow space for it, and receive it.

Now I connect down to the depth of my heart where the spirit of God has made His home–where He dwells–Him in Me. I discovered Him in the quiet of my heart, in being centered, in daring to be exactly who I am. In that still quiet space, God exists–and He was there all along.

God redeemed and restored my relationship with my mother and brought us to a place that only He could take us. After years of talking, working, and praying through all of our differences, we now understand and enjoy each other. I now consider her to be my best friend. We live together today and partnered to take care of my precious father for several years when he battled Alzheimer's Disease.

I'm incredibly grateful for the time I had with my dad. We had some special years of being "buds," connecting deeply as we walked out our journey to healing together. In the last couple of years, though he was not mentally with us many days, I could still see glimpses of his loving spirit and passion. I cherish those moments and the closeness we shared.

Alzheimer's is an evil disease. The days arrived when he declined further. Finally, we lost him just as I was putting the final touches on this book. As hard as it was, I am overwhelmed with gratitude that we shared a love so great that we were willing to do whatever it took to connect.

I'll always love him most for how he loved and supported me so beautifully even when I was at my darkest, and for how he was willing to take a hard look at his own pain to heal and restore our family. I'm grateful to the professionals for helping us through the hard times, and I'm most thankful to God for the healing and redemption that only He can do in the midst of our pain and brokenness. There is no greater gift than to enjoy your family at a deep, authentic heart level - to fully know, accept, and love each other the way we do now.

My work has transitioned into a Christian counseling and coaching practice where I empower men and women to awaken to their true identity, unlock their inner fire and power, and unleash their greatness within. I love coaching them to step into the life of meaning, purpose, and prosperity that God has for them. I help them uncage from all the mindsets and habits that hinder them personally and professionally so they can thrive in a life of freedom and fullness and make the impact they were created to in the world.

I am passionate about teaching and coaching other entrepreneurs, executives, and leaders the wisdom and practices I've learned so they are empowered to break free from the bondage of performance, people-pleasing, burden, lack, fear, and overwhelm. It's deeply rewarding to help them supercharge their success and satisfaction in life, work, and business. I also enjoy the privilege of leading and developing a team of five other like-minded and like-hearted therapists and coaches at our group practice. Together, we help adults, adolescents, children, couples, and families heal and thrive.

TRUST THE PROCESS

Transformation doesn't happen overnight. The truth is that our outer world is a reflection of our inner world. It mirrors what we feel, how we think, what we believe. Until we dedicate time every day to heart healing, maturing in our faith, and personal growth, life will always be a struggle. We must be hungry for the more that is available to us and be willing to do the inner work to expand into the brave, fierce, mighty Warrior we were intended to be.

The process is not consistently upward or linear, and it can be quite messy in the middle. Thriving in the life of freedom and fullness we were created for is achieved with small, courageous forward steps rooted in truth taken consistently over time. We don't have to have all the answers today about how it will happen, and we can't do it all at once. We simply choose to start somewhere. Wherever that is and no matter how far away you feel from what you truly want–just decide to start.

The first step may be to decide to quit the vicious cycle of striving, struggling, and surviving. If you don't know how, then ask for the help you need. Support is there for you. God is there for you. I'm here for you. All the people who love you are there for you. You have to decide you're going to start being there for you, too. So, start choosing YOU!

When I first began this journey, I had no idea what it would take to create the change I wanted because I felt so exhausted, lost, and frustrated. I simply decided that I wasn't willing to continue existing the same way I had been. I asked for help, and I surrendered to the process. Then, I began to move forward in truth, moment by moment, step by step.

Some days it was doing one thing to move me closer to what I really wanted. Other days, it was taking larger steps and seeing more significant progress. Either way, progress occurs over time as we let go of what no longer serves us and invest our time, energy, and resources into more of what makes us come alive.

We are powerful, divine beings, capable, and unlimited in our potential, but we must stop limiting ourselves. It's not about making ourselves feel better. It's about being better and having a greater impact on the world. It's about knowing who we are and what we're capable of. Instead of living half-awake, half-hearted, addicted to comfort, and settling for self-limiting mindsets and habits, we must discover and unleash our Warrior within. Then we can fight bravely, freely, and wholeheartedly for the life we were intended to live–for our destiny!

THE WARRIOR'S REWARD

The life of the Warrior is not easy. It is challenging, requiring commitment, discipline, and sacrifice, but the rewards are great.

There is no having arrived or some finish line in this story–I don't stay in a great place all of the time. Fear still tries to bully me. Expectations, people-pleasing, and performance still entangle me, and the deceiver still whispers lies into my ear.

Sometimes, it feels dark and scary, and I panic because I can't see the next step or where the road is leading. And I worry if it's going to happen for me. Will I arrive at the destiny God has for me, or will I stumble at some unexpected intersection of old habits and hurts?

But I keep coming back to my heart, to the quiet, to the beauty, to the trustworthy love of God. I keep daring to show up and be present in the chaos and the unknowns of life–in all my humanness and inadequacies.

Above all, I do not abandon my heart. It is life to me. It is where the Spirit of God resides. Only when I understand and experience God's unconditional love can I know the worth of my heart.

Today, I live as a strong woman, a brave soul with a fierce mind. I am a Warrior who, out of my power and authority in Christ, combats the darkness in my heart. I also battle darkness in the hearts of the people whom God entrusts to me to counsel and coach. Yet, I am also vulnerable and sensitive. Softly, I need, I desire, I cry, and I embrace it all.

And I will stay the course. I answer God's wooing of my heart. I accept His call to live in the beautiful story of love and restoration that He is writing in my life. Because He loves me and He is for me.

You were not made to merely struggle, strive, and survive. You were not made to live stuck in disappointment, defeat, and despair. You were created to live victoriously in an extraordinary life. You were intended to thrive in a life of freedom and fullness!

It's time to awaken to the truth that you are a powerful divine being–a son or daughter of the King–a Warrior! You have a unique purpose, a destiny to fulfill that no one else has, a special piece of God's heart that no one shares. You are chosen and beloved. You are not the lies you have believed. Your inheritance is not the life of struggle you've existed in. Every day is a battle for your heart and mind–for your very identity and your destiny.

But that's not the end. There's more. So much more.

You have a rescuer–God Himself. He dwells in you, and His Holy Spirit in you will ignite a revolution, transforming you from the inside out as you connect to your heart and to His. As you align with Him and experience His presence, He will unveil his mysteries to you, and He will reveal to you who you really are. As you connect to your true essence and do the inner heart work, the wounds and lies that have robbed you will be healed. The fuel of your passion and unique purpose will propel you forward.

You will uncage from all that blocks you from living in your most powerful self. You will throw off all that keeps you stuck in a smaller and harder existence than God intended for you.

As you know with confidence who you are and whose you are, you will see that you are not the problem and that you are enough. Supernatural courage will rise up in you. You will be empowered and equipped to step into your most powerful self–and enter the land of promise and purpose that God has for you.

Beloved Warrior, there is more for you! Open to that truth, and breathe it in. Allow it to awaken your inner fire. Your gifts make room for you in the world, and people need what you have. Draw a line in the sand today. Stop settling for mediocrity and an ordinary existence. You are a powerful creator and change maker.

You fill a special place. God is writing a beautiful story in your life like He is in mine. His love is trustworthy. The life He offers is an incredible journey.

Will you join me?

Warrior, Arise! Live bravely, freely, and authentically you! The world desperately needs what God put in you!

EPILOGUE

"I WANT TO CREATE A WORLD no one knew existed and can't live without."

When I heard this statement years ago, it ignited a fire in my heart. I immediately wrote it down and since then have kept it in sight daily as a reminder of the impact I want to make on the world. It sparked in my heart a deep desire that God wired in me as my life purpose. One of my dreams is to create a sacred place in nature–a sanctuary where animals and people come to heal, grow, and thrive!

I want to build a haven where men, women, children, families, couples, and teams come to heal their emotional wounds and powerfully transform their hearts, minds, relationships, businesses, and every area of their lives. In this special place, we will offer counseling services of all types, life and success coaching, plus seminars and workshops, half-day, full-day, and multi-day retreats for men and women on topics ranging from healing and enhancing marriage and relationships, to clarifying purpose and vision and unlocking abundance to soar in leadership and business. Movement, health, and wellness practices and therapies will also be included.

This will be a place where people can come to retreat from the noise of the world to center themselves and gain clarity. We will play, learn, and practice spiritual disciplines and experience the presence of the Lord in a real and personal way. In this peaceful, nurturing setting, we will connect with God, nature, and lots of His precious creatures. The environment will foster authentic connections and community.

For years now, I've been asking God for clarity of vision for this sanctuary, for guidance and wisdom, as well as for resources, partners, land, and favor in creating it. I recognize that this dream is way bigger than me, and that it will take a team. He has shown me pieces of His plan, but many of the details still only He knows. Building and managing a place where people and animals thrive in a life of freedom and fullness burns inside me every day. I've surrendered my dream to God, and if He wants to create it through me, I am willing and ready.

Many days, doubt knocks at the door of this big dream. I get disappointed and discouraged as it doesn't manifest in my timing or my way. Each time this happens, I may feel sad, cry, or even pitch a tantrum for a bit, but then I surrender the vision again to Him and ask for wisdom and provision.

Sometimes I cry out in discouragement, "Why, Lord, would you put this in my heart for so long and not bring it to fruition?" I know my heart is in the right place and my motive is to help people and animals heal and thrive! Why wouldn't God want to build a place like that? Sometimes comparison sets in and robs me of more hope as it often seems that God is bringing other people's dreams to fruition and not mine.

In the revision stage of this book, the burning desire to launch this plan became unbearable. My pain and desperation poured out, and for a while, it was messy and ugly. But when I relinquished it to Him yet again, I felt a release inside—a letting go—and a feeling of relief from the pressure that had been building. I simply said to God in my quiet time, "Lord, I offer myself to you. Use me however You please. I choose to trust you with my heart and my story. I know that your plans are good. Teach me to love your people well."

I felt peace inside but didn't sense anything more from Him at that time.

One morning, during my first coaching session of the day, I experienced a breakthrough. My relatively new client was smart, kind, engaging, and very enjoyable, much like all of my clients. Highly functioning and successful, his life on paper looked amazing. But on this morning, there was pain in his eyes. As he sat down and began to share, tears poured out.

"I have a great life," he said. "I'm very grateful for it, but I've been numbing my pain inside for as long as I can remember with one substance or distraction after another. I have always felt like I had to be everything everybody else needed me to be, and it's exhausting. I don't feel like I have done very well. It's never enough, and in the process, I've lost me. I feel tired, lost, and diminished."

He shared how this had played out in his life and in his work and how he struggled with the bondage of performance and people-pleasing. After several minutes of processing, he shifted.

"Over the past couple of weeks, since I've started this healing process with you, I've still felt sadness and uncomfortableness while working through some of the hard stuff that I have avoided for years, but I've also felt moments of empowerment like never before. They were distinct, and they felt right. I've never felt anything quite like it."

"In those moments, I have finally felt happy, good enough, and hopeful. I was able to be fully present with myself and in my life, and it all felt okay. It was better than any substance or distraction could ever make me feel."

"All I can say is that I am starting to feel more fully alive and that the Lord has given me a snapshot of His love and what He has for me. I can't wait to see all that's ahead. I realize that I no longer have to use things to numb or avoid my pain–and that's a freedom I've never experienced. It's the best feeling in the world, and I want more of it."

As I listened, my heart felt that familiar warm glow that I've experienced hundreds of times in sessions when clients get a taste of breakthrough freedom. That feeling is better to me than any other feeling in the world. There is nothing more rewarding than to see someone's deep pain and weariness begin to heal and transform into hope, passion, and freedom!

On this day, it was even more special. It was exhilarating to see this precious man experience breakthrough healing, hope, and freedom. I was honored and grateful to be a part of such a powerful life change. I also felt a sense of hope and freedom of my own like I hadn't felt in weeks.

God's presence was evident, and I heard His voice in my spirit.

"Con, This is what I created you for. I gave you the gift to see people–their pain and struggle–and I gave you a Warrior's heart to battle against the darkness in the world–to help my people heal and be set free from bondage–so they can live victoriously in their true identity and destiny. I put the dream in your heart for the bigger vision for a sanctuary, and it's coming. But this safe haven you create every day right here in this little office, where people feel seen, known, and loved, where you hold space for them to share their heart and their struggle–this is already a sanctuary. And you are a vessel for their healing."

Immediately, I felt a welling up of love and gratitude for the gift of my calling. Though the greater vision and the way I foresee counseling, coaching, and teaching people on a larger scale is not yet fulfilled, I trust that God is faithful to do more than I can think, dream, or imagine. Until then, I will be faithful to serve Him and to shepherd the hearts of my beloved clients in this comfy little haven of an office that He named "The Sanctuary."

Thank you, God. There is no better gift to my heart! I trust you with the More in your timing, but I will be faithful in this space and this season to love people when they can't yet love themselves. I will reflect the beauty of your heart so others can live in a world they never knew existed and now can't live without.

ACKNOWLEDGMENTS

MY HEARTFELT APPRECIATION to all of you who have fought alongside me in this beautiful journey and helped me make this happen!

To Mom and Dad: You are my heroes. I honor, cherish, and love you!

To Rusty Huddleston: Thank you for being such an incredible man after God's own heart and a treasure to mine. You're my rock!

To Joyce Beverly: I couldn't have done this without you, and I wouldn't have wanted to do it with anyone else. You are a brilliant mind with a beautiful heart. I am so thankful for yours and Cal Beverly's wisdom, guidance, and expertise. I love you both like family. Thank you for loving me so well!

ABOUT THE AUTHOR

CONNIE JONES is a therapist, life and success coach, author, and motivational speaker in Peachtree City, Georgia. She is passionate about connecting with people's hearts while engaging the unique stories they've fulfilled in their personal and professional lives.

An intuitive and dynamic motivator, Connie recognizes the barriers that prevent her clients from living in true freedom and fulfillment. She empowers them to break away from old beliefs and patterns that keep them struggling, striving, and surviving, guiding them to powerful transformation in their lives. She helps them step into their truest, most powerful selves, so they can live and lead bravely, freely, and authentically in a life they love!

Connie coaches entrepreneurs, executives, and leaders across the country to awaken their inner fire, uncage from limiting mindsets and habits, and unleash their greatness. A natural discerner, she recognizes and understands her clients' innate design and strengths as well as their internal conflicts. She guides them to discover their passion and purpose, grow in wholeness, and tear down barriers that hinder their success. Tapping into their inner wisdom and power, they experience deeper levels of meaning and fulfillment, soaring to new heights in their personal and professional lives.

As an avid blogger, vlogger, and motivational speaker, Connie imparts hope and passion to her audience as she shares wisdom from her struggles and victories. Her audiences benefit from her expertise as a highly sought after therapist and coach for more than a decade.

Connie holds a B.S. in Exercise and Sport Science from the University of Georgia, an M.A. in Sport Management from the University of Georgia, and an M.A. in Professional Counseling from Argosy University. Her professional experience spans from fitness professional, to sports performance coach to sales and management executive. She is an innovative, natural leader who is an energetic, driven, and savvy entrepreneur.

Connie lives a heart-centered, growth-minded life, fueled by passion and founded in purpose. Both a Warrior for people's hearts and a free-spirited wildflower, her life purpose is to see the beauty of God's heart and be a reflection of that to others. Connie loves people, animals, and nature, and she invests in her health through CrossFit training and running. Family and community-focused, she enjoys nothing more than seeing people Thrive in a Life of Freedom and Fullness!

Connie's specialties include:

- Counseling for Men and Women
- Life Coaching
- Executive Coaching
- Success Coaching
- Business Coaching
- Couples Counseling

- Sports Psychology
- Spiritual Discipleship

Contact Connie to book her to speak at your event, organization, or meeting. To learn more about her customized talks, workshops, and keynotes, visit www.warriorarise.com to contact Connie and start a conversation.

WORK WITH ME

I KNOW ALL TOO WELL what it's like to feel swallowed up by the endless treadmill of performance and people pleasing. I am familiar with feeling discouraged and defeated because life did not turn out as I had hoped. I have walked in the sadness and disappointment of failure and experienced the agony of a dream lost.

I have felt paralyzed by the unrelenting fear and shame that deceived and imprisoned me in a much harder and smaller existence than the one I yearned for. I have experienced the torment of overwhelming debt and financial scarcity. I have been lonely, lost in a life of expectation, burden, and obligation. I know the overwhelm of striving to do enough and have enough to be enough.

The harder I tried to get free, change my circumstances, control myself, and make life happen for me, the more frustrated and hopeless I felt. The more I worked at being noticed and approved of, the more disappointment and discontentment settled into my heart. Though it appeared to others that I was happy, popular, and successful, I felt defeated. I watched as everyone else lived the life I wanted, and I felt lost, forgotten, left out.

If this sounds familiar, I would be honored to help you escape the prison of daily despair and break free into the freedom and life God intended for you. Don't spend any more time in bondage. Don't spend another day struggling and striving. Take a first step in the direction of your destiny.

Visit www.warriorarise.com to start a conversation. Let's explore some of the many ways we can work together.

Contact me today! I can't wait to hear from you!

Made in the USA
Columbia, SC
01 November 2021